UMBANDA

The Religion of Brazil

African Spirituality and Tradition
Book 14

MONIQUE JOINER SIEDLAK

African Spirituality and Tradition Series

UMBANDA
THE RELIGION OF BRAZIL

MONIQUE JOINER SIEDLAK

OSHUN
PUBLICATIONS
oshunpublications.com

Disclaimer Notice

Please note the information contained within this document is for educational and entertainment purposes only. All effort has been executed to present accurate, up to date, reliable, complete information. No warranties of any kind are declared or implied. Readers acknowledge that the author is not engaged in the rendering of legal, financial, medical or professional advice. The content within this book has been derived from various sources. Please consult a licensed professional before attempting any techniques outlined in this book.

By reading this document, the reader agrees that under no circumstances is the author responsible for any losses, direct or indirect, that are incurred as a result of the use of the information contained within this document, including, but not limited to, errors, omissions, or inaccuracies.

Umbanda: The Religion of Brazil © Copyright 2023 by Monique Joiner Siedlak

All rights reserved

The content contained within this book may not be reproduced, duplicated or transmitted without direct written permission from the author or the publisher.

Legal Notice

This book is copyright protected. It is only for personal use. You cannot amend, distribute, sell, use, quote or paraphrase any part, or the content within this book, without the consent of the author or publisher.

ISBN: 978-1-956319-78-1 (Paperback)

ISBN: 978-1-956319-79-8 (Hardcover)

ISBN: 978-1-956319-77-4 (eBook)

Cover Design by MJS

Cover Image by @victor_tongdee and @designosaurus depositphotos.com

Oshun Publications

9 Old Kings Road STE. 123- 1038

Palm Coast, FL 32137

www.oshunpublications.com

Books in the Series

African Spirituality and Tradition

Hoodoo

Seven African Powers: The Orishas

Cooking for the Orishas

Lucumi: The Ways of Santeria

Voodoo of Louisiana

Haitian Vodou

Orishas of Trinidad

Connecting with your Ancestors

Blood Magick

The Orishas

Vodun: West Africa's Spiritual Life

Marie Laveau: Life of a Voodoo Queen

Candomblé: Dancing for the God

Contents

Introduction	xiii
Basic Beliefs and Practices for Umbanda	1
The Differences Between Umbanda and Candomblé	5
The Three Principals	15
World of the Spirits	31
Temples of Umbanda	61
Rituals and Ceremonies	65
Priests and Priestesses	69
Conclusion	77
References	83
About the Author	85
More Books by Monique	87

Introduction

Umbanda, a syncretic religion originating in Brazil, combines elements of Kardecist Spiritism, Candomblé, and Popular Catholicism. The first, Spiritism, refers to a French doctrine that originated from the thought of Hippolyte Léon Denizard Rivail, best known as Allan Kardec. Following his mediumistic studies, he postulated the existence of spirits and the soul's immortality. In fact, as he explained in his book, human beings are not morally elevated spirits who inhabit human bodies to achieve intellectual enhancement (Kardec, 1984). The second, Candomblé, is a very diffused African religion, nowadays mainly practiced in Brazil. This religion consists of the cult of Orixás divinities, defined as emanations of the unique God. They are anthropological archetypes manifest in the real world as herbs, colors, and food, providing humans with the universal energy they require to survive: the axé. The last, Popular Catholicism, refers to all religious practices that originated as cults of the Roman Catholic Church. How does Catholicism play a role in Umbanda religion? Through Candomblé. In fact, Candomblé developed in Brazil through the influence of African priests who reached the New World as enslaved people between 1549 and 1888. During this period, Portuguese Catholic missionaries converted all the enslaved Africans that did not entirely abandon their religious traditions. The Catholic Church, through colonization, specifically uprooted any form of voodooism among African populations. This defamatory campaign continued even after the Abolition Act of 1888 until it was mitigated during the Second Vatican Council, where traditional African value was recognized.

Despite the significant influence of such colonization on enslaved Africans, they never substituted their traditional folklore but progressively integrated it into the new Western religion they were forced to preach. Moreover, Brazilian slave traders were increasingly importing enslaved Africans throughout the slave trade. Their reproduction caused a demographic growth of natives in Brazil, ultimately bringing vast groups to their establishments. In fact, the spread of traditional African folklore increased all over the coastal cities of Brazil until a new cult was born in the 1950s: Umbanda. At the beginning of the 1990s, 25% of the population of 120 million were Umbanda members (Brown & Bick, 1987). However, a more recent report indicates that less than one percent of the Brazilian population claimed to belong to Umbanda and Quimbanda, a different version of Umbanda dealing with black magic and Voodoo (IBGE, 2022). A more updated account is needed to establish the current adherence rate to this religion. It is now mainly practiced in Brazil but has branches in Uruguay and some of the United States.

The historical occurrence of the Catholic conversion of enslaved people failed to eradicate African traditional beliefs. In fact, the Orixás correspond to the cult of the Catholic saints, and each Orixá has its saint counterpart. For example, the Christian God corresponds to Olorun or Zambi in the Candomblé religion. The Christian Jesus is Oxala in Candomblé, the god of creativity. All these traditions combined ultimately formed Umbanda at the end of the 19th century, which mainly spread in the Southeast part of Brazil. In this way, the Umbanda pantheon is made of a hierarchical ladder, where God occupies that highest rank and humans the lowest. Humans, however, can ascend this ladder through multiple reincarnations with which they achieve intellectual and spiritual evolutions. The figure of Olorum/Zambi comes from the African tradition. It has maintained its connotation to God in the Umbanda cult and other deities. However, the figure of Exu, still a member of African tradition, has changed its purpose to a more extreme one. Suppose Exu was originally a prankster and infamous deity (the expression of a good/evil duality) in Umbanda. In that case, Exu is sometimes defined as the Devil employed to perform curses.

Despite 'Umbanda' being a term used to indicate a combination of all the cults, as mentioned earlier, some argue that this syncretism of religions makes up the national religion of Brazil (Engler, 2012). Despite the strong African component in the Umbanda religion, members do not feel strongly about reclaiming the origin of their cult. In fact, Umbandists define their cult as closer to a Catholic tradition than an African one. They stress that all Umbanda deities embody Catholic saints only by changing their names. In this regard, their desire to be vindictive isn't strong, given that Umbanda's primary focus is happiness for all, which means it does not retain political resentment. As some priests affirmed (Roldán, 2011), Umbanda attempts to differentiate itself from Catholicism, as it always considers people's problems first rather than solely worrying about economic profits. Unlike Catholic priests. According to other sources (Lanternari, 2006), the integration of Catholic and African cults into one derives from past attempts of Umbanda practitioners to hide their worshiping, given that they had been forced to preach it in clandestinity for so long. In fact, it is evident how all the representations of

Introduction

Umbanda deities, to indicate their divinities, were mainly black-skinned martyrs and did not preserve any characteristics of classical Catholic representations.

If the roots of this religion are so multifaceted, where does the term come from? Lattuada (1989), in his book about his experience with Umbanda in Brazil, describes his conversation with Mae Divina, a priestess. The latter was taking care of his high temperature. When he asks her, "What is Umbanda?" she answers that the term Umbanda derives from Kimbanda, a Bantu priest. He was a healer, a wizard, and a fortune teller. He used to preach the meaning of Umbanda, which encompasses universal knowledge, elemental forces, and ritual objects. In Angolan etymology, Umbanda means "the art of healing," and the person who practices it is the healer. In fact, according to Batus, Umbanda is first knowledge: art, science, the expertise of curing with natural and supernatural remedies, the capacity to establish a connection between the human being and the Death's spirits, and to determine an influence from these spirits into the material world. Secondly, Umbanda is the means through which elementary forces heal the body, perform divination, and influence spirits. Thirdly, Umbanda is rituality, which ultimately allows a connection between the physical and spiritual world.

Between the 1920s and 1930s, Umbanda was mainly spread among the middle class, at that time called "Umbanda Pura," meaning "Pure Umbanda." That declination of Umbanda had stronger inclinations towards Spiritism and Occultism and greatly emphasized African deities and their worshiping. However, since its creation, this religion has undergone various developments and transformations. Among her branches there is Umbanda Kardecista, Africana, Candomblé, and Macumba. Despite the continuous effort to unify during the years, the current preachers of Umbanda have accepted the multifaceted nature of their religion and embraced it as a syncretic cult. Throughout its evolution, Umbanda still differed from Umbanda Pura since the latter focuses more on the practice of charity and a great emphasis on allowing the adherence of all members by reducing costs and increasing compatibility with their daily routine and working hours. During the first years in which Umbanda was born, it was mainly practiced in Rio de Janeiro and surrounding areas. Its initial limitation resulted from the severe repression exercised by the police of that time during the Vargas dictatorship, which urged Umbadists to organize associations to encourage political defense. During the first Umbanda Congress in 1944, the preachers expressed the intention of purifying Umbanda from all rural African customs, such as animal sacrifice and black magic rituals, to tailor Umbanda towards a noble goal. In this way, the Umbanda initiation rite differs from Candomblé's. It is simpler and does not include any sacrifice. During the initiation, Caboclos (Natives) and Preto Velhos spirits enter the initiate's body, which is in a trance, to provide guidance and assistance to the physical world. This new refinement, which separated Umbanda from its evil counterpart, Quimbada, along with the end of the Vargas Dictatorship, resulted in a significant expansion of Umbanda in all parts of Brazil. In fact, preachers grained political representations and integrated members from all casts of the population, especially while a significant migration from rural areas to the cities was occurring. All this activity contributed to making Umbanda the most practiced religion in Brazil today.

Despite the various modifications that Umbanda undertook, it is still considered a syncretic religion due to different cultures and traditions. While the general structure of Umbanda is preserved with the maintenance of Bantu deities from religions all over Africa, the integration of Orixás comes from Yoruba traditions covering western Africa, including Nigeria,

Benin Togo, and some parts of Ghana. The iconography of Umbanda is also very diverse and comes from various traditions. In fact, the only purely Bantu African figures are the Preto Velhos (Old Blacks). At the same time, the Bantu nature spirits and Bantu ancestral spirits have entirely disappeared in modern Umbanda. The concept of sacraments, liturgy, and place of a cult are all elements of Catholic inheritance.

CHAPTER ONE

Basic Beliefs and Practices for Umbanda

AT THE VERY HEART OF UMBANDA AND ITS TRADITION IS THE belief in the possibility of spiritual progress for all humankind. In particular, Umbanda envisages the world to be composed of different levels of reality, such as the spiritual and the material world. As mentioned, Umbanda's core belief has been greatly influenced by Kardecism, which integrates different schools of thought. Umbanda inherited from Kardecism the concept of intellectual and spiritual evolution, which is the only natural path that all spirits need to undergo, given that they were born ignorant and undeveloped. The key to success in this route is to practice charity and to always act for the good of others. This evolution occurs through multiple reincarnations. The already highly ranked spirits– those who have achieved intellectual elevation–need to assist the less evolved ones during their stages. This assistance is provided through the mediums, who are momentarily possessed by high spirits to guide those who have just started their journey. High spirits usually communicate through automatic writing or speech. The medium carries the spirit's message on Earth and among humans. It follows that inhabitants of the material world–

humans—are beings from the past that recurrently perform reincarnation to achieve the intellectual elevation they pursue.

Generally speaking, Umbanda's Pantheon, as mentioned earlier, is composed of a supreme God and intermediate deities called Orixás. Orixás are further subdivided into a multitude of guide spirits and protectors. These spiritual figures originate from the Yoruba tradition of Western Africa, in which they were created by Olorun to protect human existence and represent all of his power on Earth. Among the most important Orixás is Oxalá, the leader of all Orixás and embodies the Lord of light. Another is Iemanjá, who represents feminine creation, and Xango, the Lord of Justice. There are many more, each serving a specific purpose of human existence.

Another important aspect of the Umbanda religion is the worshiping of spirits. As part of the world of the Spirits, there are different levels: the Pure Spirits, the Good Spirits, and the Bad Spirits. The first group is made up of Angels, Archangels, Cherubims, and Seraphims: they are the entities that have reached spiritual perfection and ultimate elevation. These features have distinct roots in the Christian Bible and connect with Islamic and Jewish traditions. Moreover, they are comparable to Dante's Paradise in the Divine Comedy, where he inserts them into his celestial hierarchy. In Dante's work of art, Seraphims and Cherubims belong to the highest rank of angels that look directly at God and live within Him. According to Dante, the Archangels and Angels belong to the lowest choir and now take part in the creation of the Cosmos and the history of humankind. The Good Spirits represent actual figures in the Umbanda religion, as they directly enable the communication between the spiritual and material world. These spirits enter the bodies of mediums through momentary possession during public ceremonies. The Caboclos are the spirits of old deceased Brazilian natives who fulfill the role of healers: their expertise involves herbal medicines and natural remedies to assist ill individuals. The Preto Velhos–Old Blacks–embody the spirits of ancient native enslaved people who, at the time, died after being tortured and maltreated. Their function as a spirit is to teach compassion and wisdom to humans, which is a stage they were able to reach because of the suffering they experienced during their lifetime. Among other Good, Spirits are the Crianças, spirits of deceased children, and the Boiadeiros, spirits of dead cowboys. The third group is the Bad Spirits, or Kiumbas, expressions of darkness and maleficent entities. The evocation of these spirits is practiced only by Quimbanda followers, with Quimbanda being the evil correspondent of Umbanda and the religion of black magic. The only connection that Umbanda preachers have with Evil Spirits is offering them gifts to appease their bad actions. This is because Kiumbas can possess a medium's body during a ceremony; therefore, priests should always be prepared to face such circumstances. The two most important Evil Spirits are Exu and Pomba Gira; however, they can also be considered Good Spirits according to their connotations.

Exu is associated with a demonic figure, or the Devil itself, although information about this matter is quite ambiguous. According to Prandi (2001), Exu is given a double meaning. On the one hand, Exu was attributed to the identity of the Greek and Roman god Priapo. This divinity represented a little man gifted with an enormous phallus. According to the Greeks, he was the illegitimate son of Zeus and Aphrodite, and according to the Romans, that of Dionysus and Aphrodite. Exu is believed to be associated with Priapo, given the Oxira representations and phallic symbols that have been retrieved.

On the other hand, Exu was associated with the Jewish and Christian figure of the Devil, given their similar immoral characteristics. However, on this matter, there are no specific myths that directly portray Exu to be the representation of the Devil. Pomba Gira, analogous to Exu, has a double personality. She is both a good spirit that leads men on the right path by exploiting their weaknesses and an evil spirit that embodies the figure of feminine sexuality and desire in the most negative sense. It has a perverse connotation and is thought to be the guiding spirit of the "inverted" (homosexuals) and lesbians. However, according to Roldán (2011), Umbanda tolerates integrating homosexuals and transgender people. Moreover, Evil Spirits are believed to be ignorant and imperfect forces and are not particularly fought for this reason. Instead, they are ignored and kept away, as Umbanda reckons they will evolve and gradually acquire goodness and benevolence.

Generally speaking, Umbanda is a very heterogeneous religion practiced by various socio-economic castes. People seeking superficial protection to be assisted in everyday life are generally artists, politicians, and politicians. On the other hand, those who commit entirely to it are searching for constant and powerful spiritual guidance that will assist them throughout their lives. These people have generally invested with far more responsibilities than less invested followers. Umbandists have to follow a strict moral lifestyle imposed by their religion. In addition, they have to economically and practically assist the prosperity of the temples and obey paes and maes, which are the priests and priestesses of higher ranks. Devoting their life to Umbanda in such a way will allow them to operate their own temples and give them the possibility to ascend the hierarchy and become maes and paes themselves.

CHAPTER TWO

The Differences Between Umbanda and Candomblé

THE TERM 'UMBANDA' GENERALLY REFERS TO THE BRAZILIAN syncretic cult born from the combination of Christianity and African Animistic religions brought to Brazil through the slave trade. In this way, it might seem that there is no difference between Umbanda and Candomblé, as the latter religion originated from the fusion of Christianity and African tradition. However, there are fundamental differences between these two cults, especially concerning the places where these cults are practiced. Umbanda and Candomblé are Brazilian cults from African slavery from the 17th to the 19th century but developed in different religions and states. Umbanda was mainly born from the Congo-Angolan tradition of beliefs, while Candomblé started in Bahia de São Salvador. When considering the theological differences between the two cults, the differences are less prominent and mainly related to each religion's relationship with the deities. In Umbanda, communication with Orixás is established through a medium, while in Candomblé, it occurs directly. In this regard, when investigating the features of Umbanda, we cannot ignore the three main branches of Candomblé directly coming from the mother nation of the enslaved, both ethnically and linguistically speaking.

Candomblé d'Angola

Candomblé d'Angola is based on the cult of Orixás, sharing this main characteristic with Umbanda. However, the terminology used to refer to them is very different. Candomblé d'Angola names the Orixás using a vocabulary belonging to the Bantu pantheon (divinities worshiped in many African states where the primary language is Bantu). Bantu mythology was very complex, based on the existence of a single God, usually corresponding to the figure of the Sun or other fundamental natural elements. Underneath the presence of this main God, other minion deities and spirits played the role of mediators between God and humankind.

Although Candomblé and Bantu are different cults, they still share many similarities. For example, Bantu greatly influenced Candomblé d'Angola, especially from a terminological point of view. In fact, rather than talking about Olorun and Orixás, Candomblé d'Angola speaks about a high creator God named Nzambi. Underneath Nzambi are other minor deities called Minkisi, which directly come from Bantu theology. These divinities, filtered through Candomblé d'Angola, became much more similar to Orixás than traditional Bantu divinities.

Another peculiarity of Candomblé d'Angola is the special devotion reserved to specific types of spirits, the Caboclos, which will be analyzed in detail in the chapter dedicated to Umbanda's Good Spirits. The Caboclos are protective and honorable spirits belonging to the line of warriors. Before disincarnation, they were enslaved Africans before reaching the spiritual purity required to exit the reincarnation cycle. In this specific type of Candomblé, these positive spirits are considered direct ancestors of Angolan people. The fundamental deities of Candomblé d'Angola are:

- Aluvaiá, who is a mediator between humans and Minkisi (like Exu will be in Umbanda).
- Ngunzu, the protector of hunters and shepherds, and generally all people who entertain a primordial relationship with nature (like Boiadeiros for Umbanda).
- Katende, who is the most expert divinity in the field of magical and healing herbs (like Caboclos will be in Umbanda).

Candomblé Jejé

The term "Jeje," meaning "stranger," derives from the Yoruba language, an African dialect spoken by more than 50 million people. The expression Candomblé Jejé refers to a particular version of Candomblé practiced by people who, in Brazil, were considered strangers. These people were Africans from places presently known as Nigeria, Benin, and Togo. The inhabitants of these places reached Brazil during the mid-1600s and started to be called Jejes. When discussing the three principal branches of Candomblé, they are generally referred to as three different nations. Within Brazil, there would be a Bantu nation, belonging to all the Candomblé d'Angola followers speaking the Bantu language, a Jeje nation, and a Ketu nation. However, it is not about real nations or realities independent from one another, but rather, groups sharing the exact origins but different dialects. The aggregation of people forming into small "nations" resulted from Christian pastors who attempted to separate enslaved people according to their state or region of origin.

If Candomblé d'Angola comes from Bantu tradition, Candomblé Jeje has Yoruba origins. The Yorubas are an ancient ethnic group from West Africa; they were deported during the slave trade in regions of South America. Like in the case of Bantu mythology, Yoruba religion also exhibited similarities with what would have become Candomblé Jéjé. Yoruba religion is called "Santeria," based on the belief in the existence of a primordial divinity, Olorun. This is where Umbanda took the idea of Olorun as well. According to Santeria and then Candomblé Jéjé, Olorun inhabits a supernatural world. It uses intermediaries of spiritual nature, Orixás, to communicate with men. These entities are animistic in heart, including the divinity of wind, thunder, lightning, and rivers but also encompass divinities of faith and death. Each Orixás protects a specific sphere of existence and reigns over it like a guardian spirit. Moreover, an Orixá does not only reign a sphere of existence or natural elements but also protects singular individuals. In this way, the Yoruba religion thinks every human being has a referential divinity—similar to the angels in Umbanda—and can be discovered through a procedure called "the ritual of the hand." This ritual is a palm reading practiced by a Santero, a man who knows the fundamental laws of religion and the entire universe. Overall, both Yoruba and Bantu cults greatly influenced Candomblé and Umbanda, passing onto them characteristics that would have become canonical.

Candomblé Ketu

Candomblé Ketu is the most diffused in Brazil among the three branches, and like Candomblé Jéjé, has Yoruba origins. It was born, similar to other branches, after the slave trade in areas of South America. More specifically, it emerged after the settlement of Yoruba origins in the Brazilian region of Bahia.

For this reason, Candomblé Ketu represents the fundamental branch of this religion in the state of Bahia.

Candomblé Ketu distinguishes itself from the Jejé branch through ritual procedures rather than incongruencies from a religious point of view. In fact, both Candomblé Ketu and Jejé combine the traditional beliefs of the Yoruba religion with Christian beliefs, introduced after the slave trade in South America. In particular, Candomblé Ketu still maintains the Yoruba language by using it during rituals and attempts to preserve the Yoruba traditions concerning prayers, theological tales, sacrifices, and offerings. Moreover, Candomblé Ketu employs a rigid hierarchical system of power within its religion, with the highest position occupied by the Mother Priest. She is the figure who has reached the highest grade of spiritual elevation from terrestrial restraints and who has the leading role in communicating with Orixás. Next to her, we find Father Priest, who serves the same functions. These priests are elected based on their spiritual capacities, their level of expertise, and the amount of knowledge they have collected during their lifetimes.

During the slave trade, different African ethnicities were deported from Africa to South America, where they forcibly encountered and integrated principles of Western religion through Christian missionaries. Most nationalities already had referential beliefs (Bantu and Yoruba, namely) that were gradually combined with the teachings of Catholicism. In this way, the typical divinities of Bantu and Yoruba mythologies undertook different directions. The otherworldly Yoruba God was identified with the God of the Old Testament. The messengers became the angels of the Jewish tradition, and so on. Various religions were born out of this combination, presenting differences concerning terminological matters or rituals and maintaining similar theological principles.

Umbanda Esotérica

The concept of Esotericism embodies all those doctrines: Kabbalah, Gnosticism, Alchemy, and many more that practice strict secrecy of their theories and credos. The mysteries they preach are only accessible to members of those doctrines, which form proper sects. The possibility of becoming members is mainly reserved for individuals who exhibit significant intellectual elevation and intelligence, ultimately enabling them to know the absolute truth (mysteries of the universe, the truth about life on Earth, etc.). Some specific features are the use of rituals and symbols that allow communication between the different states of reality. The different roles of pupils and masters, a hierarchy in every system or sect, and the belief that nature is a living organism. This way, Esoteric Umbanda presents these elements along with the Kardecist features common to traditional Umbanda. This specific branch is usually disregarded as a ramification of Umbanda, as it incorporates more of the European tradition than the African one.

For this reason, it is called 'White Umbanda.' It is practiced by a significantly smaller portion of people. It is mainly found in smaller cities and regions of Brazil. Because this branch is greatly influenced by Catholic tradition, it is not unusual to see priests recite only Pater Noster or other exclusively Catholic songs and prayers. In Umbanda Esoterica, it is not uncommon to see a complete refusal of African traditions expressed as rejecting African iconography and symbolism. For example, Preto Velhos and Caboclos figures are depicted as European spirits, not Indigenous. The usual rituals lack traditional elements: no more orixás, food offerings, or African terminology. From these clues, Esoteric Umbanda attempts to eradicate all primitive aspects of the African tradition. As a new doctrine, Umbanda incorporates elements of astrology, palm reading, and New Age healing rituals. These New Age practices refer to all metaphysical and occultist influences incremented in religious communities. According to these doctrines, central importance is given to the concept of elevated consciousness (a synonym of spiritual awakening), which would lead to universal peace and the termination of all pain and suffering. Among the most common practices are tarot readings, psychological therapy in the most ethereal form, massages, diets, and meditative yoga.

With all this information, scholars have coined the terms "New Age Umbanda" and "New Era Umbanda" to refer to all these new elements integrated into the original syncretic cult. This new syncretism has been observed in Florianópolis, the Brazilian state of Santa Catarina. The study reported by (Oliveira & Boin, 2018) documented the practice of "Umbandaime," which is a term used to describe the exercise of Umbanda rituals accompanied by the consumption of ayahuasca (Oliveira & Boin, 2018). In a temple in Florianópolis, the investigators observed innovations concerning the food offered to the gods, characterized by the prevalence of all sorts of fruit. Another new practice followed during ceremonies was the therapy of reiki, a traditional Japanese healing method, and workshops on astral traveling and consciousness projection. Overall, this new syncretism represents the natural evolution that such an already multifaceted religion has been undertaking throughout the years. Common to the original Umbanda tradition is still the practice of charity, mutual help, and assistance among the members of the same terreiro, ultimately achieving intellectual development in one form or another.

Quimbanda

Quimbanda refers to the opposite of Umbanda and directly symbolizes the worshiping of Exu, the only Spirit the Quimbandists venerate. Quimbanda has primarily been compared to medieval and contemporary Satanism, although the two practices differ for several reasons. For instance, Quimbanda is specifically performed to cause harm, kill, and curse. Satanism, on the other hand, is usually practiced as a means to justify unorthodox sexual practices or mistreatments rather than directly inflict pain. Interestingly, when the Spirits of Quimbanda are thrown to somebody through the means of a curse, there are different outcomes to this. If the targeted person does not have enough spiritual strength and has a propensity toward negativity or having "bad fluids," they would be abducted by those spirits and be driven to commit suicide. If, on the contrary, an individual's spirit emanates "good fluids," the spirits of Quimbanda will be driven out and returned to the person who sent the curse.

Given that this person is evil for having sent the curse in the first place, they will not have the protective "fluid" to safeguard them from the action of the Quimbanda Spirits. They will become victim of their own witchcraft. The Quimbanda Spirits occupy different layers of the Astral World they inhabit. In the first layer, we find the Souls, whose leader is King Omulu. This well-documented figure corresponds to the Christian Saint Lazarus. King Omulu represents the Earth's vibration, governs the Earth's crust, and is the Lord that welcomes the spiritual bodies after their physical death. He can be defined as the Lord of death and can be invoked to put an end to things or radically change them. Among the other layers, we find different dimensions, always led by Exus of a different nature and rank. A few examples are the layer of the Skulls, led by João or Exu Caveira, and are the first spirits in contact with the death's words; the Nagô layer is led by Exu Gêrêrê and is the line of knowledge. Their expertise concerns the art of Voodoo and curses, and they are explicitly invoked for this purpose. All these spirits inhabit the deepest layer of the Astral World and correspond to Hell (otherwise known as Inferno), which is analogous to the Christian tradition. This place is made of a viscous substance. Like Dante's description in his Divine Comedy, it is also inhabited by the souls of people who were vile and meant during their lifetime. The actual Black Magic and witchcraft belong to another Spirit's world, which lies next to the Inferno. It is another part of the Astral World. It is inhabited by the Shadow's spirits, the darkest entities of cemeteries, such as worms feeding on the cadavers' flesh. When they throw their curses, they are the quimbandeiros alleys, and they will induce the victim to lose all their vital force. The victim's body will acquire a yellow-green ill-like color, lose all physical strength, and be haunted by a feeling and desire for death.

Quimbanda's origins are not well documented, but it is thought to have been born when Umbanda began to seek its own independence from any black magic cult. This happened in the 1940s when Umbanda reclaimed its identity and detached itself from voodooism and animal sacrifice (Giumbelli & Almeida, 2021). Quimbanda is mainly practiced in the Rio Grande do Sul, compared to other Brazilian states. Unlike Umbanda, Quimbanda did not evolve since its creation. This is because it is a cult more than a religion and is practiced in the suburbs and outskirts of Brazilian cities. It is an obscure art performed in secrecy and turned away by most people that are fascinated yet terrified by it. Depending on the magnitude of the curse, different animals are sacrificed. For more straightforward procedures that cause little harm, Quimbanda offers chickens or small goats. For more complex and specific curses, the sacrifices can involve larger animals like oxen or bulls and are even thought to involve human sacrifice. The costs of a Quimbanda ritual are very high. They must cover the practice itself and the objects used to perform it: the candles, the animals, the alguidar (a terracotta plate), and others.

CHAPTER THREE
The Three Principals

The Pantheon

SUPPOSE UMBANDA IS A SYNCRETIC RELIGION COMBINING beliefs from different cultures. In that case, the cult of Orixás is a purely African tradition. In fact, the adoration of these deities comes from the Yoruba people. They are one of Nigeria's most prevalent ethnic groups, with more than nine million people claiming to be Yoruba. The foundational concepts and beliefs that Umbanda preaches in cults come from the Yoruba people. From Yorubas, they inherited the belief that the world is either all evil or all good. The Orixás are essentially the representation of all the good parts of the world. For this reason, they must be adored and worshiped. They are representations of truth, human features, and characteristics, and, importantly, they were once humans before becoming deities.

To understand Umbanda's complex set of beliefs, one must consider the intangible nature of the universe. Umbandistas are unable to make sense of it and believe no humans can. However, Umbanda attempts to make sense of the universe and give it meaning by fragmenting it into infinite parts that are comprehensible to human intelligence. The ultimate, incomprehensible omnipotent God is Olorun, the creator of the universe. He corresponds to the Christian conception of God. He is responsible for the creation of humanity on Earth and all cosmological phenomena (such as rain, sun, wind, and fire). He is also responsible for establishing laws and punishment for human intellect and ultimate death; that is, the end of all things. Despite his greatness, humans are not required to worship and revere him, as he cannot be contained nor even conceived by the human brain. Because there is no connection between him and humankind, he is inaccessible and has no need for any adoration; however, he is continuously responsible for human life and death.

Given that he embodies the infinite universe, humans need to fragment him into many different parts to conceive his existence. In this way, Olorun is distributed into smaller pieces, the Orixás, and each expresses a characteristic of Olorun that is comprehensible to human intellect. However, this practice of fragmentation only reflects Umbanda's attempt and all African religious branches where Olorun is present to understand the nature of the world and give sense to human existence. The work of Romanian religious historian Mircea Eliade has described Olorun as an unconcerned, uncaring, remote, sluggish, and essentially absent entity (Eliade, 1961). On the other hand, in many African religions, God is considered far away and close to humans. This concept is expressed by the African description "Andro Androa." People from Lugbara, in central Sudan, use this expression to mean God is sometimes close and sometimes far because his greatness allows him to choose his position and accessibility.

Given that Orixás are extensions of one unified God, Umbanda can be considered a monotheistic cult since their adoration is a means through which they express love and devotion to Olorun. Specific to Umbanda's belief and different from Candomblé and Batuque, the main Orixás are seven, given that this number symbolically fuses the physical matter, represented by the number four, and the spiritual world, represented by the number three. Despite being separated from Animism, Umbanda posits Olorun is, paradoxically, an all-human and non-human form, both organic and non-organic. In this way, every human, plant, animal, and object contains a tiny portion of Olorun's energy.

Oxalá (Oxaguian/Oxalufan)

Oxalá corresponds to the Christian figure of Jesus Christ and embodies the Holy Trinity, composed of the Son, the Father, and the Holy Spirit. It is the most significant extension of Olorun. It is sometimes interchangeable with Olorun, who is equally responsible for creating the Orixás, the world, humankind, and nature. Oxalá represents everything good and pure in the universe. Umbanda's Oxalá differs from the Yoruba traditional pantheon, where Oxalá balances out the good and the evil. For Umbanda, it is purely good. If Olorun is unreachable to humans and not worshiped, Oxalá is praised as the god of all Orixás and humans.

Oxalá is the first invoked deity regarding the benediction of life, home, family, and loved ones. He is addressed on Fridays and Sundays while all lunar phases promise to appeal to him. Sunrise and twilight are preferred times to say prayers or perform rituals. During rituals in his honor, Umbandistas give him white flowers, such as lilies. Following tradition, scent the environment with orange blossoms. Given his high-ranked position among the Orixás, priests and priestesses use golden objects and gemstones during the ceremonies. The precious stones are extracted from diamonds and white crystals, and their white and milky colors represent symbols of purity and holiness. He is ultimately the most worshiped Orixá in

Umbanda, given that he gifted humans with the power of free will. We have basil, marcela, jasmine, and pear trees among his herbs and plants powered by him. These herbs are generally used for infusions in cold water. According to tradition, Oxála had two wives. One was Naná, with whom he gave birth to Iansã, the goddess of wind and storms, and the other Omulu, the god of sickness and physical bodies.

Iemanjá

The figure of Iemanjá comes from Candomblé tradition, corresponding to Yemaya from West Yoruba, and is considered the goddess and nurturer of all Orixás. Like all other Orixás, she is linked to the Catholic tradition and corresponds to the Virgin Mary. However, she is quite a different character in African and Brazilian traditions. She is originally a water goddess and mythological figure representing the Niger River. When the figure of Yemaya reached Brazil, these people turned her into the goddess of the sea. This mutation derived from a legend narrating that Iemanjá, in an attempt to run away from her husband, she left the river and reached the sea to reunite with her mother. Because of this transformation, Brazilian culture refers to her as the protector of Indigenous water spirits, where she has been extensively depicted as a mermaid who protects sailors and fishermen. Concerning her day of worshiping, in Rio de Janeiro and São Paulo, she is celebrated on December eighth, while in Bahia, she is celebrated on February second. According to the legend surrounding her, Iemanjá was a curvy woman with big breasts and the guardian of water, a symbol of life and birth. One day Olofi, the king of Ifé, proposed to her. She accepted on one condition; that he would not love her for her sensuality and objectify her based on that. He promised to never make any allusions to her big breasts and love her for her spirit and inner beauty. However, one day, when Olofi got really drunk, he started sexually harassing Iemanjá by complimenting her breasts and, in this way, breached their promise.

As a consequence, the queen ran away. Olofi, regretting his action, chased after her. Iemanjá did not hesitate to break the bottle her mother gave her, which contained a magic liquid that would turn her into a river and drag her away. Olofi then turned into a hill to block her way. Xangô, Iemanjá's favorite son, hurled a bolt to break the hill in two and let the river pass. Iemanjá ultimately refused to return to Earth and decided that her forever home would be the water.

Xangô

Xangô is the Orixá of Justice and embodies righteousness, balance, order, and wisdom. He can be compared to the Greek God Zeus and his Roman correspondence, Jupiter. Xangô is one of the most venerated Orixá, and his symbolism transcends human justice. In fact, he represents what is right on a universal level rather than on human laws and regulations. He also embodies the concept of relative justice. This means that something might be right and fair today but not tomorrow. Comparative justice also differentiates between what is right for the individual and humankind. In this regard, Xangô would always choose universal good rather than favoring personal pleasures.

For example, the death of an individual might cause suffering for their relatives. However, on a universal level, it is good, as it allows human progress and development through the life-death cycle. Furthermore, Xangô needs to transcend human laws because they are time and space dependent, given that they change with time and from place to place. As an expression of relative justice, Xangô's symbol is the two-bladed ax. Xangô also represents the universal clock (symbolizing universal time) compared to human conceptions of time governed by people. He also embodies institutions, governments, states, and stability. His sense of peace extends to the familial realm, in which he personifies the paternal and patriarchal figure as he is authoritative, strong, and has a firm sense of honor. As a mythological figure, he has multiple women, such as Obá and Iansã. He is also a frightening Orixá when upset, and his natural symbols are fire and thunder, as recalled by a myth.

Xangô, in fact, is surrounded by a mystic and sinister legend. Such legend traces his whole story, from when he was an inhabitant of the material realm until his ascension to the Orixás world. During his terrestrial life, Xangô was the king of Oyò, an ancient Nigerian city now inhabited by Yoruba people. The reign of Oyò had been a matter of rivalry between Xangô and Ogúm, another famous Orixá. This rivalry lasted until Oxalufá, a very old Orixá, proclaimed Xangô as the king of Oyò by gifting him a necklace with six alternated white and red pearls. As soon as Xangô became king, he showed off a belligerent character. He was always at war with surrounding populations and would consistently defeat them. He was so strong and powerful that, one day, two heroes from the conquered cities came to his door and asked him to teach them the art of war. Xangô, worried that someone could pass him in ability, taught them the bare minimum and did not reveal his deepest secrets. However, whatever Xangô disclosed to them was enough for the two heroes to become extremely strong warriors. This caused Xangô to become vengeful, as he declared war upon them. The two heroes were appalled. They announced to Xangô and the Oyò ministers that they would have rather died than fight the man who taught them all they knew about war. Xangô, upset, ordered them to be burnt in a fire, but the flames had no effect on their skin. Instead, he commanded that they walk on hot coals, but their feet did not feel any pain. Lastly, he ordered them to be thrown into a cauldron filled with hot oil, but their bodies did not feel any different from a bath in the sea. Xangô was humiliated for his intention to harm others out of envy and vengeance, so instead, he vanished into nothingness under the shocked gaze of an entire crowd. That day, Xangô became an Orixá, albeit an upset one. He threw pain and humiliation onto Earth and caused earthquakes, storms, and other catastrophes. In this way, humans started to give him offerings and ceremonies to calm his fury, which managed to tailor his negative characteristics into good ones. His talent for war made him a wise entity and, eventually, the king of justice.

Oxúm

In most civilizations and cultures that worship gods, there is always a deity that represents water. This is because sea and lake water determine progress and prosperity for civilizations. Lake and river water indicate that humans and animals of a tribe can flourish because they have water to drink, wash with, irrigate the camps, and harvest: it is ultimately a symbol of physical health. This can be exemplified by looking at how significant civilizations developed by an important river. For example, Egyptians evolved by the Nile, whereas Mesopotamian civilization expanded by the Tigris and Euphrates. Seawater points to economic wealth, as it allows trading goods and traveling and facilitates communication with surrounding populations. Umbanda has different water deities, such as Iemanjá and Oxúm. This deity is very different from the figure of Pomba Gira, given that Oxúm embodies the innocence and naivety of physical love and highlights its natural and spontaneous side. With Oxúm, there is no sign of sin and transgression. She is linked to the idea that life can only be possible through physical procreation, as she fully embodies this concept. She is beautiful and charming and can be compared to the Greek goddess Aphrodite. A synonym to address her is "Yeyè," which means 'sweet mother,' since birth and conception are attributed to her will. In fact, ceremonies and rituals to spur family and offspring are practiced in her honor. Her symbol is water, and it's linked to Oxúm's capacity to promote plant and food growth. It also refers to her ability to wash away all of the Earth's impurities linked to evil. Oxúm, like all other Orixás, can be bad to those who disrespect her. Genitalia and intestinal diseases are among the harms she can inflict.

Ogúm

Ogúm is the god of war, iron, metallurgy, and all manual work related to this field. He is the protective spirit of the Nigerian river Ogun, which runs from the Sepeteri Oyo State to the Lagos State. Ogúm takes his name exactly from this river. He embodies human progress, advancement, and development and is a master of problem-solving, practical resolutions, and instinctive action. He can overcome every issue and obstacle and is a brave and fearless entity: he is the Orixá of victory. His symbol is the sword, but it has different connotations. Besides symbolizing strength, it also refers to the phallic instance of penetration. This does not strictly allude to penetration but entails entering the substance of things and objects and changing their forms. The myth surrounding this figure tells the peculiar love story between Ogúm and his first wife, Iansã. According to the legend, the two were tremendously in love and had similar characteristics. Iansã was strong, combative, and the perfect partner for the fearless Ogúm. The two, however, could not manage to give birth to any son, as Ogúm was only capable of fragmenting the matter and not fertilizing it. In this way, in an outburst of jealousy, thinking that she could be loved by someone else, he fragmented her into nine pieces with his sword. This gave birth to nine different versions of Iansã, which could be added to form a more complex version of her.

The Umbandists protected by this Orixás have characteristics similar to him. They are emotionally hardened and consider emotions to be superficial and evil flaws that need suppression and control. They are also physically strong and are typically athletes, runners, fighters, and proficient workers. They have a rigorous lifestyle, which includes not drinking alcohol and engaging in reckless behavior.

Oxóssi

Oxóssi is the god of hunting and, along with Ogúm and Elegbará, form part of the triad of war deities. If Ogúm has the characteristic of being instinctive in his problem-solving abilities, Oxóssi is the exact opposite. He is strategic, introspective, and reflective and embodies attributes of satiety and wealth. Being a hunter, he is patient and quiet and always waits for the perfect moment to attack. He is a simpler Orixás in comparison to others and their characteristics. In fact, his role does not indicate complex metaphors–like the fragmentation of matter–but instead connotes a specific yet essential element of human existence: nutrition. Performing rituals in his honor means praying for an unlimited food supply, the absence of famine and starvation, and ensuring proper nutrition with enough proteins, carbohydrates, and vitamins to sustain life.

Interestingly, he also plays a role in the syncretization between African cults and Indigenous divinities, which makes up the cult of the Caboclos in Brazil. The Caboclos are important entities since they are part of the Good Spirits, possessing mediums during rituals. The Caboclos are the spirits of deceased Indios who became divinities and are still worshiped in the Umbanda cult. Oxóssi is the leader of the Caboclos, and they are both invoked through rituals inside forests. They are especially needed to solve problems regarding special intelligence and strategy and health problems involving nutritional deficits.

Ibeji

Ibeji is a peculiar figure worshiped in Umbanda. This is because Ibeji is represented by two twins, as depicted in all Umbanda and Candomblé statues dedicated to them. The reason for this double personification is the symbol they embody: they represent the birth of all the children in the world and, by extension, the conception of all things. They also symbolize pure joy and happiness for the beginning of life. The legend surrounding their figure narrates they are the sons of Xangô and Iansã, who abandoned them on the shores of a river right after their birth. They were found by Oxúm, who heard their cries and came to their rescue. The story tells that as soon as Oxum looked at the babies' faces, they smiled at her, and her heart filled with a sense of purification and serenity. Like all the other Orixás, the Ibeji lived on Earth as human beings before becoming deities. The Ibejis were two children, two princes, that were considered wise because they saw life in simple ways: through the eyes of a child. They were consulted to solve problems whenever the solution needed was too simple for adult perception. However, one day, as the two children played by a river and during one of their pranks, one child fell into the river and drowned to death. Because they were inseparable and the living child was suffering too much for the death of his brother, Orunmila–the Orixá of divination–turned them both into Orixás. To comfort everyone for their disappearance from the human world, Orunmila left two statues of the children by the river. Even today, the statues remain present in the Umbanda cult during rituals organized in honor of the Ibejis. The people protected by these Orixás are essentially eternal children. Suppose the Ibejis are considered wise for their infantile approach to life. In that case, the people they watch are regarded as those who need constant support in their life choices. Because of their childlike nature, these people tend to ignore all sorts of responsibilities and dump them onto others. They are sometimes frivolous and prefer light-hearted mundanity over the monotony of a rigorous lifestyle. They can also be selfish and capricious like children are when they refuse to share their toys. Overall, their cult was born from the desire to deify infant mortality, which was common in the twentieth century. The idea of the statues as a means to represent the Ibejis was born from the belief that the children's spirit could be enclosed in that object and, through it, live forever.

Omulu/Obaluayê

Omulu or Obaluayê is the deity of diseases and death. For this reason, it is a feared Orixá for Umbandists. Like all other Orixás, he exemplifies a complex and tumultuous personality. He has the power to heal the world from diseases and, in contrast, fill it with pandemics and death. According to legend, when Olorun was distributing special forces to all Orixás, Omulu received characteristics of sexuality, making him the embodiment of this human feature present in all men. However, Omulu was not a suitable carrier of such a feature, as he used it to have intercourse with many women. Orulun was outraged when he realized that Omulu was engaging in such behavior. For this reason, God condemned Omulu to death by syphilis. In this way, he became the god of diseases, as he could either protect humankind from them or cause deadly pandemics if upset. This makes him a multifaceted deity, as he can use his power for good or bad outcomes. Worshiping Omulu does not only represent a way to ask for protection and health but an attempt to understand death and revere it as a part of human life. Since humans feel lonely and lost in front of death and have no power to influence its course, the only thing they can do is integrate it into everyday life. Omulu's followers and worshippers have great awareness of the existence of death. They understand that death forms part of a bigger picture and that one must not fear it. Worshiping Omulu also means accepting death as part of the bigger picture in which man exists and of which it is impossible to reach the boundaries. According to currents of thought, Omulu is one of Exu's manifestations and hence a bearer of evil and malice. However, being the embodiment of "death" does not imply negative connotations since Umbandists understand its importance for Earth's development.

Iansã

Iansã is the goddess of the wind, storms, and general meteorological conditions. She corresponds to Saint Barbara in the Catholic tradition and is one of the wives of Xangô. She is the most rebellious and reckless Orixás, especially among women. She is brave, strong, competitive, and the most prone to anger. Her liaison with Ogúm was very important to determine her characteristics as an Orixá. In fact, she embodies the concept of versatility, mutation, and change according to the mutations of the universe. Each of the nine fragmented pieces of her represents a version in which she is whole. These nine versions also represent the nine deltas of the Niger River. They are linked to the different phases of human existence. Among these are youth, adulthood, and old age, which occupy the greatest part. In relation to Xangô, there are three versions of their story together.

According to the first, Iansã stole the secret of lightning and fire from Xangô so that she could master controlling natural phenomena. According to the second, Xangô loved her so much that he shared with her his secrets. Lastly, the third version narrates that when Xangô sent her to find a potion containing all those secrets, she drank from it out of curiosity. This made her aware of all the potion's mysteries, and Xangô became dependent on her to discover such secrets. Contrary to the other female Orixás encountered until now, she represents the feminist Orixá, who refuses and fights male authority.

She wants and seeks a leading role for herself rather than simply being a wife of an important Orixá. Finally, she is the most unpredictable Orixás, like the natural phenomena she controls. In this way, Umbandistas not only pray for her to receive advantages but to keep her calm and well-disposed. Her main symbol is the machete, demonstrating her leadership and temperament as she rules a masculine object.

Nanã

Nanã is the most ancient of all Orixás, and she is considered the mother of the Earth. The symbols linked to this Orixás are mud, rain, the stagnant water of swamps, and the trees' roots. Despite seeming like a sinister figure at first glance, she is a pivotal Orixá who embodies the Earth's fertility. In fact, nature requires wet mud to grow its seeds, and rain is what nourishes the soil and allows the harvest to flourish. She is the guardian of life at its bare roots; she is ancestral, and without her, the first glimpse of life would not have been possible. Her creative force allowed the birth of all civilizations and humankind by extension. Everything that was once born through her will eventually return to her at the end of all things. Her name means "root," and in Umbanda tradition, she is portrayed as an old and wise lady. In fact, she represents the archetypical old lady whose features are dignity, kindness, and wisdom. She is also a symbol of womanhood and matriarchy, embodying the feminine duty of giving birth to children and taking care of them. She depicts a woman's journey and the many forms a woman can take. She is an image of sexuality and lust, but also a nurturer and a mother.

The energy of this Orixá does not necessarily cause life or death but assists humans during these moments. For example, when a person leaves the physical world because of death, she intervenes to calm their heart and spirit by alleviating suffering. She frees the person's mind from all the memories in the moments preceding the end of a heartbeat. More broadly, the calming and slowing energy of Nanã serves other scopes in everyday life. For instance, she assists humans when they need to free their minds from intricate thinking and helps relax the nerves to promote clear and rational thought. This is required when a situation of change and separation is about to occur, as extreme as life and death and as simple as a life choice or circumstantial problem.

Oxumaré

Oxumaré is the Orixá that is a bridge to all things of life. More specifically, he is the deity that allows the continuity of the cycle of life and determines the connection between the sky and Earth. Economically, he is also a carrier of prosperity and richness. According to the legend surrounding this figure, Oxumaré was a babalao—a very high-ranked priest—and served king Oni at his court. Despite his well-known wisdom and intelligence, Oni did not treat Oxumaré with respect and was hostile to him, making him live a life of deprivation and poverty. One day, Olokum, the governor of land close by, called Oxumaré at his court to assist his son, who was extremely sick and helpless. Due to the babalao's extreme intelligence and resourcefulness, he found the remedy that saved Olokum's son.

For this reason, Olokum gifted him all sorts of riches and spread the word about Oxumaré's talent. When the now rich babalao returned to Oni's court, the king was furious. He worried someone else could take the babalao's talent away from him. His court, so he gave him even more wealth. However, it was too late. Oxumaré had already been summoned by Olorun, the supreme God, who called him to cure a deadly ocular disease he had developed. When Oxumaré managed to cure the supreme God, the latter did not allow him to return to Earth among humans more than once every three years. It is believed that when Oxumaré visits Earth for a short period, he descends through a rainbow cloak, bringing prosperity and joy everywhere.

All these features, especially the concept of his frequent journeys to Earth through a fictitious bridge, feed his image as a connector between worlds. His symbol is the ouroboros, the snake that bites its tail in a circle, representing life's circularity and movement. He does not only connect the sky and Earth but also brings together all the Orixás to human reach and functions as a bridge between Olorun and humankind. This Orixá also brings the message of success in life, which is made possible through perseverance and the constant exercise of the human brain even during hard times, like his at Oni's court.

CHAPTER FOUR

World of the Spirits

Pure Spirits

THE FIGURES REPRESENTING THE PURE SPIRITS HAVE THEIR origins in the Bible. Suppose the Orixás world is an expression of the African influence in Umbanda. In that case, the world of the spirits is its Catholic counterpart.

Angels

The figure of the Angel belongs to the Bible, and many interpretations have been provided to explain their role in the world. The topic of angels has been addressed in different domains, spanning Christian philosophy of the fifth century, such as the work of Pseudo-Dionysius the Areopagite, until more recent works of the twentieth century, such as Klee's paintings or Rilke's elegies.

Overall, it seems angels are "ministers" of God. On one side, they bring messages to men through apparitions; on the other, they contemplate and glorify the Lord. According to famous Italian philosopher and critic Giorgio Agamben, angels' greatest role is to address God's personality. Given that angels are the messengers of God and carriers of His word, studying them allows us to investigate the nature of God Himself. This question has been raised among many religions, such as Christianity, Judaism, and Islam. The primary intent is to understand if God is a Deus otiosus, a lazy and detached God, extraneous to humans—like the case of Olorum for Umbanda—or if He is a present figure that takes part in human existence.

Christianity, Judaism, and Islam have answered in their own way. The rabbis, for instance, initially minimized the importance of angels in acknowledging their roles. God created them to perform specific roles as if they were guardians of justice. According to Aristotle, God exercises his will and power on Earth through the angels, showing his nature as a present God who partakes in the life of humans.

Umbanda inherits the concept of angels as guides and ministers of God. It shifts it towards a role purely tailored toward the good of humans. For Umbanda, angels are mentors who constantly follow the human to which they are assigned to guide them towards righteousness. They are omnipresent beings who can hear and see everything happening on Earth. However, rather than having a protective role, they are more like advisers, which is why in Umbanda, the word 'angel' is synonymous with 'mentor.' Like the Good Spirits, angels were present on Earth several lifetimes ago. However, unlike the Good Spirits, they likely had a special relationship with the person they guarded, such as a relative or a friend. To honor the relationship with their angels, Umbandists light a candle next to a glass of water and pray to receive good qualities, such as intuition, intelligence, rationality, and the promotion of a human connection to God.

Among Umbanda, angels are a particular category composed of Elemental angels. Elementals are spirits that embody natural elements such as fire, Earth, water, and air. Unlike other Umbanda figures, these spirits are not present in different forms and only fluctuate in the element they govern. Their form is not physical, as they have not mutated in other beings; instead, it is energetical and vibrational. According to Umbanda, angels are the elementals of the fourth of the four elements: Aether. They are expressions of this element that manifests as an aural form between the physical and metaphysical realms. These types of angels are beings that fluctuate in Aether and, unlike the angels mentioned earlier, have been and are constantly present in everyone's life, transcending the familiar bond and making it universal. The more these types of angels are worshiped, the more enlightenment, protection, and clairvoyance humans will receive. By connecting to a specific element, the person creates a bridge between the element they are worshiping and themselves. In Umbanda, spirit migration is always present: all spirits on Earth will experience life in another form. These elemental angels will migrate inside the realm they belong, Aether, which is not in human form.

Archangels

The figures of Archangels are first nominated in the biblical tradition. More specifically, they are first found in the Book of Enoch, an apocryphal text that speaks about Enoch's travels. Enoch is an otherworldly patriarch who, during his quests, is accompanied by four archangels. As the name suggests, the archangels have the power to rule over other angels: they are of the highest and purest nature and the most powerful angels. They are originally Michael, Uriel, Gabriel, and Raphael (in other books, the archangels are seven and not four).

Michael is known to be God's right arm. His main role is to assist the forces of good during God's fight against rebel angels. Other traditions also mention a direct battle against Satan. The main symbol of this archangel is the scale, as he weighs the sins of men and dispenses the right dose of justice accordingly. In fact, this archangel passed into history as the guardian angel of exorcisms and of the fight against Satan.

The second archangel is Uriel, who has often been presented as a cherubim in the Christian tradition, a guardian angel at the doors of Heaven. The cherubims are peculiar entities and have been described in the Bible in many different ways. As we will see in the following paragraph, cherubims have also been described as having four faces: one of a human, the second a horse, the third a noble lion, and the fourth a bull. Uriel's symbol is the sword, and his role includes protecting Heaven and supernatural places.

The third archangel is Gabriel, present in the Book of Enoch, Judaean, Christian, and Muslim books. He is often described as the Angel of death. He also has the role of the scribe; in fact, in the prophet Daniel's book, Gabriel announces Judgment Day's arrival to men.

The fourth archangel is Raphael, who is considered to be the guardian angel of conjugal love and, in general, of couples. In this way, he has the role of protecting all the couples present in the Old and New Testament and preventing them from committing sins and falling into temptation, thereby becoming victims of Satan's power.

Umbanda integrates these biblical figures among the group of Pure Spirits, considered the most spiritually elevated beings inside the hierarchy. In the following paragraphs, when talking about Good Spirits, the concept of spiritual ranking will be clearer. Overall, the archangels are pure spirits who have never incarnated. Next, in the hierarchy, we find the good spirits, who have an elevated spiritual energy but have also been reincarnated into human bodies and then disincarnated due to their enhanced spiritual elevation. Last, we find the evil spirits occupying the lowest rank in the spiritual universe. These last spirits were once incarnated, and now, in the form of spirits, they still need to incarnate. This would allow them to act upon the world and own fragile bodies through which they can directly operate in the physical world.

Cherubims and Seraphims in the Bible

Although the word 'cherubim' has extensive associations with angels, and their meaning suggests something similar to them, the Bible presents different information. In the Bible, cherubims are first encountered when Adam and Eve approach the tree of life. However, this Genesis passage does not provide extensive details on these figures. The only thing explained is how cherubims were the guardians of the tree of life and the protectors of a sword that Adam had to dislocate to reach the tree. Despite many translations reporting the word 'angels,' the Hebrew version only presents the word 'cherubim.' However, this begs the question: why are these cherubims sitting in front of the tree of life? Indeed, there is no information about their form, shape, size, and general nature. In later passages of the Bible, such as in Exodus and The Book of Kings, cherubims are described as golden-winged statues made by craftsmen to be placed in sanctuaries. However, Ezekiel and his vision provide the most detailed description of these creatures. He saw them as living creatures coming out of a cloud; they had four faces, one human and the other three having varying animals. Despite Ezekiel's vision of introducing the cherubims as living creatures, he specifies that he recognized them as symbols of God's glory and omnipotence. This differs from the image of Gabriel, who visits Mary in Nazareth. Overall, in the Bible, it seems that cherubims, contrary to angels, are not living beings but symbols of God that appear in dreams or sanctuaries as carved objects.

Regarding seraphims, the Bible provides more mixed information. According to Isaiah's vision, seraphims were beings with six wings that preached the greatness of God. They were able to take guilt and sin away from humans by touching their lips with burning coal. On the other hand, in other places in the Bible, seraphims are described as toxic snakes used by God to castigate Israelites. Despite the ambiguity surrounding their forms, both cherubims and seraphims seem to be messengers of God. In the case of Ezekiel, for instance, it looks as if Cherubims reminds him of God's frightening omnipotence. Both cherubims and seraphims have judgemental roles through hot coals; however, most of all, they have the role of devotion and constantly remind humans of God's presence. According to Carlill (2013, pp. 205), these figures have an apotropaic function: their main goal is to keep away evil forces and cancel their malignant influx.

Cherubims and Seraphims in Umbanda

In the Umbanda cult, the adoration of these biblical figures is exhibited through the establishment of the Nigerian Holy Order of Cherubim and Seraphim Church Movement. This religious movement was founded by Moses Orimolade, a member of the Anglican Church of a Nigerian state. His family registered him to join the Church due to his unusual physical conditions; he did not learn to walk or stand up by himself until age five. Orimolade has exhibited unusual behavior ever since he was a young child. As soon as he learned to walk, Moses preached to God at night by himself while singing in front of the altar. During his adolescence, he converted to Christianity following a vision and a period of confinement lasting seven years. Given his devotion to the Church from such a young age, everyone welcomed him with pleasure and respect. Some people even summoned him to receive assistance.

Umbanda

One day, Orimolade was called by the family of Christianah Abiodun Akinsowon, a Christian girl who had a profoundly spiritual experience. In fact, according to the girl, right after the Corpus Domini ritual, she saw an angel who walked her home and spoke to her about the celestial realm. However, what was most disturbing was how the angel told her she would die if she did not meet a man of the Church. Therefore, her parents called Orimolade, who managed to heal her from her shock and ensuing hysteria. In this way, the interaction between the two gave birth to a new society born on September 9th, 1925, which worshiped the Christian figures of cherubims and seraphims.

Baianos

In Umbanda, the Baianos are one group of Good Spirits who, in contrast with the Pure Spirits, were once personified beings who walked the Earth as humans. When disembodied from their physical form, they assist humans on Earth during their spiritual journey and facilitate their everyday life. As good spirits, they have specific characteristics that differentiate them from other entities, such as having a good temperament while also being honest and severe in their judgments. When invoked, they surround the summoner with a positive and luminous aura. Despite seeming like simple characters at first glance, they are pretty intricate. In fact, their language and ability to communicate with humans through mediums is complex yet accessible if one pays enough attention. Their period of disembodiment is very recent compared to the ancient Orixás, for example. In this way, the Baianos are the spirits of the North-East population, representing deceased people who, during their life on Earth, had proven to be humble and determined.

Linha is the first Baiano and is considered the Bahia state's guardian spirit. Her role, however, is more complex. She is the guardian spirit of the sertanejo population, which are people who developed their identity based on the existence of the Bahia state. More specifically, Linha is not a guardian spirit with a national identity but rather the protector of all people who, through their actions, contributed to the birth and development of the state.

As previously mentioned, Baianos are Good Spirits who symbolize the positivity of journey and research. They have great hope and faith in humankind. They believe that, through the practice of Umbanda, humans will be able to love and respect each other like life companions and siblings. Although of a different nature, they belong to the same family of Orixás and, according to tradition, evolve their language and capacity to communicate when they possess a medium. Every time Baiano enters a medium's body, they will be more comprehensible, making them talented interlocutors in the spiritual realm. Despite their recent disincarnation, they are not weak spirits. Instead, they can push evil spirits away and reject negative energy from people who want to prevail over others.

Boiadeiros

The Boiadeiros form another category of Good Spirits and, similarly to the Baianos, have peculiar characteristics that distinguish them from other impure spirits. Therefore, the Boiadeiros, like the Baianos, have a strange relationship with humans. As spiritual and disembodied entities, they can establish communication with incarnated entities. In all their descriptions and representations, these spirits appear as spirits of nature. More specifically, they are the spirits of the countryside and pastoralism. They have a special relationship with nature and are in strict contact with the Earth and the vital cycles of the universe. Their propensity and closeness towards nature is explained by their identity during human life: they were experts on country life, animal habits, and behavior. They were in complete harmony with the Earth and nature in its purest form. Despite their disincarnation, they have not lost any memory of their human life. Even their memory is of a pure state; they remember their bond to human life and, for this reason, have the special capacity to assist humans during their path towards liberation from limiting situations, obsessive behaviors, and evil energies. In contrast to the Baianos, they also can offer support to disincarnated spirits.

The Boiadeiros reserve a special name for men who have departed from a straight and narrow path of love: they call them 'oxes.' Oxes represent herbs, which function as a metaphor to describe people whose vision is obscured by the attachment to material and economic goods. Therefore, the Boiadeiros' role works by guiding humans as shepherds do with herds. They search for these people among crowds to reroute them towards a path of love and religion and save their souls from damnation. In contrast to the Baianos, these spirits do not have a great propensity for verbal communication and narration. In fact, their relationship to humans is expressed in terms of the body's memory; that is, memory as an ancestral bond between body and nature, as well as purity of heart. Another fascinating detail about these spirits is that they were musicians during their lifetime—viola musicians, specifically. Their iconography in the Umbanda cult is their representation as cowboys. They also acquire a specific symbology. They are portrayed as cowboys with the rope that, when spun, enters the trajectory of cosmic time and enables them to retrieve damned souls in every corner of the universe, even in the most remote ones.

Caboclos

The Caboclos are part of the third lineage of the disincarnated spirits. If the Boiadeiros are a lineage of shepherds, the Caboclos are known to be a race of fighters. The Caboclos are known for their great nobility of soul, bravery, and loyalty. The Caboclo, during his life on Earth and before disincarnation, was a man of mixed race: half white and half black. However, his spiritual inclination towards loyalty and bravery is thought to have been inherited from his Indigenous side. Caboclos are also good advisors; however, they are simple in their communication style and extraneous to verbal complexity. They were also like this during their human life. Caboclos were the advisors of their tribes, known for their attachment and respect for their traditions.

Some disincarnated spirits have a special relationship with natural remedies and healing magic. In the same way, Caboclos have a fundamental knowledge and expertise of the art of shamanism. More specifically, they are experts in the art of healing through powerful herbs. Their favorite instruments are the pipes and herbal baths because they believe these instruments promote spiritual truth. The Caboclos are generally subdivided into groups, among which other spirits exist. Some of them include:

- Caboclos de Iansã (Maìra, Bartira, Ivotice, Jussara, Jurema, Japotira, Poti, Talina…). These are Caboclos that deal with manual work.
- Caboclos de Iemanjá (Estrela, Guaraciaba, Jandira, Jacira, Diloé…). These are Caboclos that tend to push away negative spirits.
- Caboclos de Nanã (Muraquitan, Janira, Assucena, Luana…). In contrast with others, these spirits do not

have a particular propensity for dancing. They are strict and noble figures and deal with Karma.
- Caboclos de Omulu (Juruema, Juruena, Araguaia…). They deal with personality issues, ranging from desperation to depression.
- Caboclos de Oxóssi (Arruada, Jupiasso, Javari, Mata Virgem…). These are disincarnated spirits who deal with the use of healing herbs. Their favorite instrument is the pipe, which they use to connect with humans.
- Caboclos de Xangô (Sete Luas, Treme-Terra, Mirim, Cholapur). They deal with everything concerning justice and righteousness.

Crianças/Erês

The Crianças/Erês have a particular story among those in the world of Good Spirits. They are considered young men or children who have not undergone incarnation due to their absolute purity. During rituals and ceremonies, these spirits are thought to play the role of intermediaries between Orixás and their child devotees. Their personality as spirits link to their young age: since they have not undergone incarnation and have not exposed their soul to terrestrial sin, their consciousness is entirely pure, spotless, and devoid of maliciousness. Another feature of the Erês, due to their youth, is their ability to speak directly. Their communication style sometimes represents a challenge for adults, who are used to more complex language. The Erês' questions are sometimes considered inconvenient and inappropriate but are nevertheless necessary to achieve salvation. These spirits are also passionate about play and dance; they love eating sweets and delicacies and, like many other good spirits, play the role of intermediaries between Orixás and their umbandistas.

But what is peculiar about the Erês in the Umbanda cult? First, they come from the Oxumaré race, the rainbow cobra. Like Oxumaré, they also have a special relationship with the sinuous movement that leads to freedom and spiritual purity: they embody the possibility of achieving fullness and freedom. The celebrations dedicated to the Erês occur during particular festivities, those in honor of Saint Cosimo and Damiao. These two last figures of Saints were doctors during their lifetime and are thought to have gifted lots of sweets and treats to children after visiting them. Overall, the Erês are fundamental in Umbanda due to their connection with kids and ability to introduce them to the religion.

Exu (as a Good Spirit)

Exu is a very ambiguous figure in the world of spirits. In the Umbanda cult, he is polymorphic and vague. On the one hand, he is considered the hyperbolic figure of evil and spiritual damnation. On the other, he is a positive figure sometimes associated with the Christian tradition of Saint Antoin.

Similar to the Erês and other Good Spirits, he has the role of an intermediary: he is a mediator between the Orixás and human beings during propitiatory rituals. Being multifaceted, he is the guardian of journeys and trades and all those situations involving wit. He is very similar to the figure of the messenger in the religions of ancient Greece (Ermes, for instance, is very similar to Exu). Exu is also the guardian spirit of fertility and wealth. It is no coincidence that he is represented as a man with an enormous phallus, which serves as a metaphor for the big dimensions of Earth and the origins of life. In this way, he reveals himself as both a good spirit and a tricky one, as he is sometimes prone to inducing perceptive deception. There are different stories about him. A famous legend surrounding this figure portrays the concept of perceptive deception, which he utilizes to teach a lesson on relativism. The legend goes as follows: one day, Exu arrived in a small village and walked on the main street wearing a beautiful and flamboyant hat. Some village residents perceived the hat as red, while others perceived it as black. In no time, a big argument ensued among the residents concerning its color. Exu intervened to show them that the hat was both red and black and that the color they saw depended on one's personal perspective. His intention was to explain how the universe is governed by multiple points of view and how pointless it was to argue over the existence of absolute truth. The day dedicated to Exu is Monday, and his sacred symbols are children's toys, coins, and turtles.

Marujos or Marinheiros

The Marujos or Maninheiros are positive spiritual entities with a special relationship with water. In particular, the Marujos have a connection with the mysteries of the sea and a special ability to communicate directly with the Orixás. In contrast with all the others, the figure of these spirits did not have a terrestrial life before his disincarnation. In fact, he spent all his life sailing on the water. Perhaps he was a sailor, a fisherman, or a pirate. In any case, he was a man whose house was water, which enabled him to establish a connection with existence. The sea was the element that helped the Marujo, during life, to get rid of all negative energies. As spirits do, he assists humans by letting them throw their worries and preoccupations into the sea. All bad energies are carried by the spirit at the bottom of the sea, where they vanish and can no longer reach humanity.

Despite Marujo seeming like a straightforward spirit, he encountered many difficulties in his journey towards liberation. The sea and the oceans are dangerous and threatening elements governed by the multifaceted and susceptible Orixás. Suffice to think of Iansã's typhoons and Ogúm's currents. Some Marujos are at the service of Omulu, assisting him with the transition from life to death. Moreover, Marujos are very peculiar spirits, as they walk staggeringly and do not exhibit outstanding balance due to their constant life on the boat and the movements of the waves. During rituals, the invocation of the Marujo occurs through the assimilation of alcohol by the medium. This is because this spirit tends to absorb a large quantity of energy and, by filling the body with a protective layer of alcohol, makes it possible for the Marujo to suck on the alcohol sugars rather than the natural ones.

Preto Velho

The Preto Velho is a positive spirit devoted to developing love, positive energies, charity, and the forgiveness of humans regardless of their actions. Unlike other spirits, the Preto Velho did not have to go through struggles to disincarnate due to their closeness to the spiritual realm during their lifetime. The Preto Velho is generally associated with ancient native ancestors. Given that he was enslaved during his life on Earth, he is still devoted to servitude during his spiritual passage. He teaches humans the importance of humility, which is a fundamental element in establishing a pure connection with nature and the inhabitants of Earth. He has a special relationship with smoking and medical herbs. In fact, through special herbs put inside pipes, the Preto Velho can trap all the negative energies of whoever smokes it during a ritual in his honor. He is also a spirit devoted to coffee, usually consumed while invoking him.

The Preto Velho is also an ambiguous spirit since he has dangerous characteristics. In fact, given his extreme power, he sometimes struggles to find balance. His forces, in this way, are usually expressed as contrasting energies inside a human; on the one hand, the person can be extremely kind and generous, and on the other, he can be subject to depression and low moods. Because he is a powerful force, the person who hosts his energies must be extremely well-balanced from the start. Some of his characteristics are sometimes syncretically compared to Jesus Christ. What links these two beings is their proneness to forgiveness. On one side, we have Jesus Christ as the inventor of absolution. Conversely, Preto Velho's message entails the divulgation of forgiveness among men.

The personified version of the Preto Velho is that of older men and women who dispense their wisdom and kindness. This spirit is also very disciplined and rigid. Because he believes in the power of preaching and teaching, assimilation of his doctrine is a challenging and complex task that meticulous men can only achieve. However, the main trait of his personality is humbleness. In fact, Preto Velhos teaches modesty to all his followers. For this reason, they are actual figures for connecting with the spiritual realm.

Preto Velho and Spiritism

The great diversity and multiplicity of syncretic Brazilian cults, especially Umbanda, integrate theories of spiritism. Such approaches are combined with Indigenous beliefs and Christian traditions from Umbanda itself. In this regard, it is necessary to mention the relationship between the spirits of Preto Velhos and astrology, which is generally known to be the study of zodiac signs.

Every person has a zodiac sign protected by a specific Preto Velho. For instance, Aries is guarded by the Preto Velho Antonio de Ângulo, which assists and rescues Aries when it shows impatience. Taurus is assisted by Vô Venâncio, a Preto Velho that provides its sign with infinite loyalty and protection. The patron of Gemini is Vò Severina, which gives its sign concentration, problem-solving skills, and perseverance. Individuals born under Cancer are protected by Tia Maria, who helps with the overcoming of loneliness and isolation. Lios are protected by Grandpa Augusto, who gives them abnormal strength and a lot of physical health. Virgo's protector is Grandpa Cipriano, who equips them with the capacity for self-acceptance and acceptance of others, regardless of their personality. Then, there is Libra, protected by Tia Pulquéria, who gives them the faculty of never doubting their choices. Scorpio is supported by Grandma Sabina, who frees the people she protects from all feelings of suffering and pain. Sagittarius is protected by Vò Cambinda, who gives them the qualities of ethics and religious faith. And last, we have Capricorn, Pisces, and Aquarius. The first is supported by Jacob, the spirit of patience and endurance. The second is held by Tia Luzia, the spirit of servilism and obsequiousness. The third is governed by Pai Chico de Aruanda, a spirit that gives freedom of spirit.

Zé Pilintra

Zé Pilintra is a positive spirit representing human beings who have faced civil and societal injustices throughout their lives. He is a very appreciated spirit among Umbandists and, similar to Preto Velho, is a teacher of humbleness and forgiveness. He is also a preacher of righteousness, as he teaches his devotees how to approach other people in the best way without stigmatizing the poor and rejected. Nevertheless, despite his appearance as a simple and quiet spirit, Zé Pilintra loves attending chaotic and busy places and is considered a great and talented dancer. Like other Good Spirits, he was confronted with a lot of suffering during his terrestrial life. This led him to re-evaluate people who are not strong enough to stand up for themselves. During his terrestrial life, Zé Pilintra was a man who suffered from isolation. Whenever he would ask someone for help, they'd simply disregard him. He was a pariah, subject to criticism, mockery, and ridicule. Once disincarnated, however, he disintegrated all negative feelings of hatred towards societies that treated him in such a way. On the contrary, he developed genuine kindness to help those who faced the same hardships as him. In Umbanda, he is depicted as a smiling spirit whose aim is to brighten up the life of those who worship him.

Let us retrace the story of Zé Pilintra to better frame his personality as a spirit. He was born in the small village of Bodocó and, as a young man, learned how tiring a nomadic life was. His village was destroyed by a heat wave. He was forced, along with his family, to find another home. But his bad luck did not end there: right after the journey, his entire family was killed by a disease, and he was left by himself, lonely and desperate. He then started to live by harbors, begging for food and shelter. However, they are always refused by others. Despite everyone's hostility, Zé had several abilities: he was an expert in the use of blades and knives, and he was very capable of defending himself from dangers. One day he decided to reach the big city, Rio de Janeiro, where he lived in the poorest and most crowded neighborhoods. He developed a passion for the community, chaos, and popular lifestyles there. He also developed an addiction to gambling and women: legend says that, with his great charm, he managed to seduce all the women he met during his life.

While conducting this life, he started to help the poor living in Rio de Janeiro. However, he was soon assassinated due to the bad friends he had bonded with. His talent with the knife was a double-edged sword. On one side, it allowed him to defend himself for such a long time, and on the other, it caused him to attract many enemies. Similarly, his spiritual identity is double-sided. He is adored in the rituals of the Shadows–in honor of Exu–and in the practices of the Light–those in honor of all the other Orixás. He is now a spirit adored by the whole of Rio de Janeiro. He soon became part of the national cinematography culture: it is enough to think of the famous movie City of God, where the main character, an expert on knives, women, and life on the streets, likes to be called Zé.

Pomba Gira

Pomba Gira is another important and famous disincarnated spirit in the Umbanda cult. She is also present in the religion of Candomblé, in which she represents a spirit whose role is to communicate Orixás' messages to the world of humans. Initially, she was considered an entity of masculine nature (called Bombogiro), but this concept soon changed. She was then associated with Exu in his most negative version. Pomba Gira, inheriting most of Exu's traits, was quickly thought to be connected with sensual pleasures, body attributes, lust, and malice. Throughout the years, her image was transformed. It became that of a woman who loved to showcase her beauty and features with the purpose of alluring men and gaining power over their lives and souls. However, her characteristics do not necessarily make her a negative spirit. In fact, she uses her influence to exploit the weakness of incarnated men to direct them toward the correct path.

The story of Pomba Gira is fascinating, as it also integrates romantic nuances. It is thought that anyone asking for her protection receives many privileges. This is because Pomba Gira, like all other Good Spirits, had a terrestrial life before her disincarnation. During that period, she had been maltreated and forced to live on the margins of society. It is a very similar story to that of Zé and other positive spirits, all of whom descend from men's and women's bodies who had a tough life of poverty and marginalization. This element is another inheritance of Christianity, where the 'saint,' the good spirit, is an entity who has suffered extensively and undergone unimaginable pain during their lifetime.

In the same way, according to Christianity, prostitutes were considered sacred, such as Mary Magdalene, who was sanctified. This tendency of hallowing prostitutes was also inherited by Fyodor Dostoevsky in the 19 century: in his book Crime and Punishment, the prostitute Sonjia, daughter of a drunken man, is the figure who helps the main character, Raskol'nikov, to develop feelings of compassion and kindness. The same concept applies to Umbanda. According to Umbanda priests, Pomba Gira is a mingled spirit that contains the souls of poor women who, during their lifetime, were forced to work as prostitutes due to poverty or difficult family circumstances. After disincarnation, these souls were combined in the figure of Pomba Gira, who, despite maintaining some links with the sexual sphere, is also linked to compassion and help.

Pomba Gira is also regarded as the goddess of love whose functions relate to protecting sexuality and romantic feelings. Comparing Pomba Gira with Exu, both are partially considered protective spirits of family environments and the relationships between parents and children. In Umbanda, Pomba Gira is depicted as a woman with beautiful and colorful clothes, wide necklaces, and floral patterns. In this way, when offerings are made to Pomba Gira, they are usually objects and things that she prefers over others: alcoholic beverages, general ornaments, big earrings, jewels, clothes, and opulent lipsticks. They are ultimately elements that reflect her great personality.

THE KIUMBAS ARE the evil spirits diametrically opposed to all the positive entities we have encountered until now. According to Umbanda, if the Good Spirits are beings who support life on Earth in one way or another, the Kiumbas produce evil for the sake of evil. These are spirits dedicated to harm, negativity, and bewitchment. They are entertained by such practices and love causing chaos within communities. The Kiumbas form a big group of evil spirits, and they live in a place called Umbras. They are invoked by Quimbanda's shamans and all people fond of black magic spells and curses. Umbanda shamans also invoked them, who are very powerful and spiritually strong. They haunt these evil spirits to find and defeat them. They do so by imprisoning them in the bodies of chosen people, which is the only way to prevent them from doing harm. For haunting to be successful, the shamans need to imprison the evil spirit in the body of a chosen victim. The process of incarnation that Kiumbas, when found, are forced to undergo is a fundamental part of the purification journey. In fact, when such spirits are confined into a body, they are confronted with feelings of suffering and constriction, which is what causes their atonement and purification.

The incarnated Kiumbas need to be recognized through specific characteristics. The body possessed by a Kiumba will be frivolous, arrogant, and devoted to violence. Their physical features include weird and unusual facial mimicry, loud yells, and protruding eyes. Their eating habits are equally abnormal: they tend to eat raw meat and hot peppers without feeling any pain and are addicted to alcohol and chain smoking. Their voices are low and hoarse. They are lustful, gossipy, shameless, and devoted to all forms of aestheticism. They are deceptive, misleading, selfish, and always ready to show off.

In addition to all the external features that Kiumbas exhibit, many other peculiar characteristics make them evil spirits. While these entities are characterized by eternal features such as the exhibition of narcissistic behaviors, yells and screams, and the tendency to show off, they are also characterized by their role in the formation of toxic internal traits. such as the formation of personal obsessions. The negative spirits do not only incarnate in someone's body to cause disarray in the external world. Still, they wish to cause turmoil in someone's internal body. The host body of a Kiumba will develop psychological disturbances, such as paranoia and obsessions. For this reason, Umbanda believes psychological obsessions result from the presence of an evil spirit who has taken possession of the body's original soul. Umbanda also conceives different habits; however, the reason one spirit might generate a given obsession and not a different one is still unclear.

First, there is the simple obsession; it is exhibited by speaking over someone to prevent them from talking. This is an important characteristic that allows us to recognize someone affected by this condition. For example, suppose a participant, during a ritual, suddenly begins shouting and playing the drums over a medium, trying to deliver important information. In that case, the participant is thought to be possessed by an evil spirit. This type of obsession is of a simple nature, tailored to generate mayhem and noise.

The second obsession is thought to be more feared in Umbanda. It is exhibited by the spirit's behavior of persuading a person's mind. Therefore, it is not only of a physical nature, as it does not produce noise like the simple obsession. Instead, it is mainly psychological because it depends on the evil spirit's mental manipulation. For example, a man affected by this obsession, who previously cared about the wealth of his terreiro and holy family, might suddenly consider these things trivial and senseless. He might begin to squander the money reserved for the terreiro for his own pleasures, thereby displaying how suddenly he has changed from the inside.

For this reason, these sudden personality changes are often attributed to the possession of a fascinating spirit, which generates this type of obsession. This obsession is generally considered more dangerous and prone to attacking weaker individuals. Still, in reality, it can penetrate any person's mind. In fact, it can assault fathers, mothers, sons, brothers, old priests, and priestesses. Ultimately, this obsession is more dangerous and hard to chase away.

The third obsession explored is the worst of them all. With this obsession, the victim is manipulated not only by the evil entity's fascination but also through the spirit's strength and physical power. The name of this obsession is called "subjugation." Employing violence, the evil spirits possess an individual's free will and make him a puppet. Once this occurs, the evil spirit can drive a man to commit robbery, violent crimes, and even suicide. The obsession with subjugation is the worst and most threatening because it is untreatable. In fact, once a spirit takes possession of a man, it is impossible to chase them away without causing serious harm to the possessed. The only way to subjugate the power of the evil spirit and chase it away from the body it possesses is by having a positive spirit intervene.

Among the Kiumbas are disincarnated, evil spirits who do not like to incarnate and possess terrestrial bodies. They prefer to invade specific places and are obsessed with people or objects of the terrestrial world. There are evil spirits who obsessively haunt domestic places. In this case, this entails a spirit who has disembodied a long time ago and keeps returning to the place they had lived in, such as a house. The spirit would torment the new tenants, hoping to make them leave their old homes. Although these spirits are annoying, they are not dangerous. Instead, they wish to return to life and be welcomed in their old house. This kind of spirit is obsessed with the memory of the life and feels nostalgia for their past life, their loved ones, and the joy they felt while alive.

Other evil spirits tend to get obsessed over a person. This occurs when it feels a particular psychological affinity for an individual with similar personality traits as them or general syntony. These spirits are typically egregious and envious and tend to bond with humans with these characteristics. The spirit starts to follow their chosen person and feeds on their negative personality. Because of this feeding, the spirit can involuntarily help the person get rid of their anger since the spirit constantly sucks it up. However, because of the spirit's obsessive nature, it will always generate anger and rage inside the person and, in this way, will always feed on this.

Other spirits are extremely obsessive but not necessarily harmful. These are spirits who are victims of romantic obsessions. During their terrestrial life, they had been tremendously in love with a person. After death, they did overcome their feelings. Because of the suffering they endured by being separated from their loved ones, they would keep obsessing over them. This obsession does not depend on the victim but on the spirit, who cannot detach itself from them. The connection between the evil spirit and the loved person lasts until this last one dies. The spirit would then lose contact with the person and continue living with loneliness and suffering forever. The spirit would then be connected with the loved one until this last one dies, to continue living a disincarnated life of pain and suffering.

Other obsessive but not harmful spirits include those who, during their terrestrial life, had been victims of addiction, such as drugs, alcohol, gambling, fights, frequenting brothels, and other behaviors Umbanda condemns as belonging to the evil world. They have still not overcome these obsessions during their disincarnated life as spirits and, therefore, continually indulge in these behaviors. They haunt brothels, bars, and casinos without realizing they have disincarnated.

Another category of evil spirits includes dangerous entities whose primary goal is to confront people who do good for others. They are extremely rageous spirits who have accumulated all their negative and toxic traits during a previous life and want to release them onto the world. They gossip, are violent, start fights, and cheat. Moreover, they are known for being smart and calculating; they spend several years studying a chosen individual to identify their weak spots and exacerbate them. They will, in fact, strike on those same weak spots to be sure their victims will perish.

The last spirits that must be mentioned are those affected by the revenge obsession, considered the absolute worst and most dangerous. It concerns the revenge of a spirit who, during life, had been a victim of an injustice. These disincarnated spirits remember everything from their past life, including all the bad things that happened to them. In fact, they will remember all the pain and suffering they endured as if they were in their disincarnated life. Because of this, they will look for revenge. The target of their retaliation will be the person who caused them pain, likely because they were abandoned or hurt by them in some way.

Exu (as a Bad Spirit)

We have already addressed the figure of Exu in the paragraph dedicated to Good Spirits, in which we said that Exu is a multifaceted spirit with multiple associations and personalities. He is sometimes thought to be of good nature; however, according to other versions, he is also compared to the Christian figure of Satan and, therefore, also considered an evil spirit. It is not the first time we've encountered a comparison between Christian deities and Umbandist Orixás. In fact, if Oxalá was compared to Jesus Christ– the most benevolent spirit–it is also natural to find a Christian comparison to an evil spirit. This comparison with the Devil occurred later when Exu had already been worshiped and adored as a positive deity in Umbanda. According to his positive connotation, he is the divinity of messages and relationships between the terrestrial and the spiritual world of Orixás. He was also thought to be the god of abundance, symbolized by the image of an enormous phallus. However, since Exu had been compared to the Christian devil, many cults' dedication to him suddenly changed. Initially, the act of possession of this spirit during a ritual was regarded in a positive light, representing the will of a spirit to teach humans. However, after Exu acquired a double connotation, possessions from this spirit were suddenly considered evil manifestations. More specifically, it symbolized a punishment issued by an Orixá to criticize a man who had sinned.

In Umbanda, the cult of Exu underwent significant transformations. For example, after the identification of Exu as an evil spirit, a new pantheon was born: the "leftist pantheon" or "pantheon of shadows," which became a fundamental element of the religious structure of Umbanda. In this way, a separation occurred: on one side, we have the good Orixás, which we have extensively touched upon, and on the other, we find the Exus (followers of Exu). These are incredibly deplorable and disincarnated spirits of people who, in life, had been rapists, murderers, thieves, and other horrendous characters. According to some versions, Pomba Giras are sometimes considered descendants of the pantheon of shadows despite playing regulative and therapeutic roles in human relationships.

For this reason, to maintain the double nature of Exu and Pomba Gira, Umbanda does not restrict them to a purely negative role. They are still given the possibility of spiritual elevation and reaching the perfection that righteous spirits have (for righteous spirits, it is intended the spirits of light).

This notion contrasts with other syncretic religions that tend to strictly separate good spirits from bad ones.

In Umbanda, all Exus followers are given the possibility to redeem themselves so they can become part of the righteous side. There is a wide versatility in all spirits' characteristics that do not frame them in an entirely good or bad light. The same occurs in Exu's case; his negative version can be attributed to a past life and the good version to a disincarnated and elevated one.

Reincarnation

The concept of reincarnation is as ancient as the world is. It is a belief shared by many cults and religions around the globe in different historical periods and locations. For instance, the Vedic religion (now known as Hinduism) believed in reincarnation. It made it the central point of their philosophical and religious beliefs. Other doctrinal preachings of this philosophy are Buddhism, Pythagorism, Platonism, and nearly all philosophical schools of ancient Greece. Each of them developed the notion of reincarnation in their own way. It is, therefore, necessary to discuss this philosophy more generally by mentioning doctrines that, through their combination during the years of slave trades, fused into what we know now as the Umbanda religion.

Christianity is certainly the first doctrine that requires attention. Although it does not explicitly explain the notion of reincarnation, it nevertheless relays a key concept: the soul's immortality. According to Christianism, one of the significant influences of Umbanda, the soul is eternal but does not reincarnate: it can either be saved or damned; it reaches heaven or perishes in hell. Death is the turning point at which the soul exits the circle of existence. In this way, these two concepts are opposed to each other: on one side is reincarnation, and on the other is the soul's immortality. It is important to differentiate these two concepts as it is not unusual to confuse them.

On the one hand, religions like the Egyptian, the Christian, and the Mesopotamic, think of the soul as an immortal entity. They consider the soul a spiritual entity, not a physical feature. According to them, the soul is a feature gifted by God to distinguish humans from animals. On the other hand, we have cults that, along with affirming the soul's immortality, state another important fact: the spiritual realm to which the soul belongs is connected to the physical dimension through matter. Before reaching its ultimate spiritual essence, the soul needs to reincarnate multiple times to achieve purification. This same principle has been declined in many religions and in various forms. Despite some terminological differences, the basic concept of Buddhism and Hinduism is the same. The soul incarnates and, through multiple phases of reincarnation, pays the prince for all its sins until it reaches absolute purification and exits the vicious cycle of eternal suffering. But, if Umbanda's main principles are influenced by the basic doctrines of Christianity, how is it possible that they exhibit diametrically opposed ideas in this regard? Well, not quite. We already know that Umbanda is a peculiar doctrine.

In turn, Christianity owes many of its principles to Plato's philosophy of the Forms (Ideas) and the One (God). The main topic of Plato's Republic Book X is the soul's reincarnation. That is where we find the Fates, or the Parche, holding the threads of fate and living in a big valley by the scores of the river Lethe. This river is special; whoever drinks from it will forgive everything that happened to them in their previous life. In this valley, multiple souls of deceased people wander, and they are omniscient. However, before they can reincarnate, they are forced to drink the river water so they can forget all of their knowledge. This explains how the Christian doctrine of the soul's immortality, derived from Plato's philosophy, is linked to the concept of reincarnation.

Umbanda does not only derive from Christianity; a significant part of its roots come from ancient African animistic cults (such as Bantu and Yoruba religions, for example). These cults thought that nature was inhabited by spirits who governed the world. These spirits were everywhere, even in the smallest blade of grass or drop of water. According to these animistic cults, man has a similar role to the rest of the beings inhabiting the world. In fact, man is not regarded as the only entity owning a soul because animals and all sorts of other creatures have one. Also, man is not the sole being split into two (between the soul and the body), and he does not even have a direct relationship with God, who is always detached from human affairs on Earth. In this way, many Umbanda beliefs can be explained.

On the one hand, Umbanda carries the influence of Christian dualism and the distinction between the spiritual and material realms. On the other hand, it follows the guidelines of animistic cults and the idea that the world is populated by good and bad spirits. With all these influences, Umbanda symbolizes the great tragedy that man has always faced in history: man is a spiritual being, tending to purity and elevation, but he is trapped in a physical body that forces him to experience passion, violence, and death.

Umbanda has two fundamental ideals concerning reincarnation.

The first one is cosmological. The world we know is only an intermediary phase, a material layer between other spiritual planes that will one day be entirely revealed to humans. Therefore, from a cosmological point of view, the world itself is subject to a process of reincarnation: it moves from a material realm to a spiritual one, going through phases, and following a path that will, one day, lead to universal perfection.

The second one is anthropological (which means it strictly concerns man). On the material plane, the spirit is forced to incarnate inside bodies. As long as a spirit inhabits a body, it will be considered impure and mixed with the sin of materiality and will always be forced to reincarnate until the fulfillment of absolute purity: the overshooting of the terrestrial dimension.

When we discussed Umbanda's Good Spirits, they were indeed disincarnated. They had reached a very elevated grade of perfection and could free themselves from their material bodies. They were elevated beyond the level of existence of ordinary mortals. With this, we can understand the importance of the medium in the Umbanda cult. The medium has reached some degree of spiritual perfection but is not elevated enough to disincarnate. They have the possibility of communicating with pure spirits. Then, being the body owner, they will be responsible for spreading the spirits' words and teachings to men. Reincarnation is the fundamental commandment of Umbanda because it explains all the procedures carried out during rituals that, without reincarnation, would be pointless. Why would you go through the struggle of invoking Orixás if this would not serve the ultimate purpose of the purification of the soul through multiple reincarnations?

The purification of the soul can occur in different ways. Here is where we reconsider the influence of Christianity in Umbanda. The fundamental difference between Hebraism and Christianity is the following. According to the first, you can only achieve elevation if you respect the law; according to the second, you can only elevate if you love, respect, and help others. Evidently, Umbanda follows the guidelines of the second: most of Umbanda's disembodied spirits were poor and maltreated people who experienced desperation and isolation during their lifetimes. This is similar to what happened to Jesus Christ. One day Jesus, in Cesarea di Filippo, realized that God's promises of achieving the Kingdom of Heaven on Earth were not being fulfilled and that the terrestrial world was not changing accordingly. Jesus concluded that Earth could not be saved physically but spiritually. His revolutionary decision entails humankind could only be saved through the embodiment of humanity's suffering within the figure of Christ. Umbanda follows the same principle. Compassion, sacrifice, and helping others are all fundamental concepts to elevating one's spirit towards higher dimensions. However, these ideas derive from the Lamb of God principles, which derive from Christianity.

All these Christian influences proceed hand in hand with African animistic cults (like Yoruba and Bantu): the respect towards spirits, rituals, and offerings in their honor, and all the ceremonial procedures that, eventually, characterize the Umbanda cult. The following can be affirmed: Umbanda preaches reincarnation by extending the Christian principles of the soul's immortality. Being the latter of platonic origin, Umbanda fuses them with animistic-pantheistic beliefs of the regional cults.

CHAPTER FIVE
Temples of Umbanda

Tiendas or Terreiros

THE RITUALITY OF UMBANDA IS A PARTICULARLY FOLKLORISTIC and peculiar tradition. It reflects all the African ethnic influences it collected in Brazil. When speaking about places of worship, known as "terreiros," we must remember that these structures and shapes were inspired by the Yoruba and Bantu autochthonous tradition, based on their geographical and ethical origins.

We have also briefly mentioned the Yoruba tradition, which will be fundamental to understanding the essential structure of Candomblé and Umbanda's places of worship. According to the Yoruba cult, the two main divinities are Obatalá on one side–the deity of the Sky–and Oduduá on the other–the protector and Creator of the Earth. When these two entities breed, their union is thought to generate the Earth, ready to be fertilized and cultivated, and the sky will host all the climatic phenomena we know to exist. The union between these two deities is metaphorized through the image of a pumpkin cut into two pieces, which can only become a whole pumpkin when the two halves are restored together. Yoruba places of worship are made of the main structure, the temple (also known as the "home"), and a long pole on one side lodged in the floor and protracted towards the sky. Such an arrangement symbolizes the sexual intercourse between Obatalá and Oduduá. Therefore, the place of worship in Yoruba tradition is structured according to the theological model, reflecting the primordial divine union. From this conception, Umbanda and Candomblé developed their own places of worship.

Here, such as in the Yoruba tradition, we see how a place of worship corresponds to and reflects a cosmological realm. This should, in turn, replicate the whole spiritual dimension through a metaphorical reproduction by means of a terrestrial place, the terreiro itself. In Umbanda and Candomblé, they do not speak about Obatalá and Oduduá. However, the cardinal principle remains the same. In this way, the terreiros are structured around a pole that connects the energy of the Earth with that of the sky and represents their union. The terreiros are thought and built to reproduce the image of a typical ancient African village. Considering the presence of the sacralized pole, there also are other constructions that remind us of the typical temple of the Yoruba cult. These objects can be fountains, usually placed in the temples to perform a purification before the start of the rituals. They can also be small houses, which are thought to be the Orixás' residencies, so they can manifest during the rituals through a medium. At the center of the terreiro is a specific space dedicated to the tradition of initiation. This space is cleaned and cleared before the start of each ritual. For instance, the floor is brushed, and they check for the presence of poisonous insects or snakes, given that interferences can influence the outcome of the ritual and the concentration of the medium when they call Orixás. The fundamental rituals of the

Umbanda religion occur within the structures of these terreiros.

The rituals occur in several different phases. The first phase sees the occurrence of purification through fountains and their water. This procedure is a clear reminder of the role of water in the Christian tradition; that is, water is an element that represents purification against evil and sin from Giovanni Battista until Jesus Christ. The second phase is usually called "the coming of the sacred spirits," which is requested and begged for by playing the percussion and the big drums. This is the pivotal moment of the whole ritual, which can either succeed or fail. In fact, this is the promising moment for spirits to descend and take possession of the medium's body. This is where the tribal dances start. Those who dance are the spirits that have taken possession of the medium's body and have momentarily entered the physical dimension because of the supplications. After the ritual dance, all spirits leave and retrieve to their celestial homes, which are still precluded to humans who have not yet encountered disincarnation. After the ritual and the effort every member has put into the call, they can all rest and regain their energies: this is the moment when the fest phase begins.

Even this moment is dedicated to the devotion of the Orixás because the mediums' bodies regain the energies lost during the possession. Only after recovering and reacquiring their energies the mediums can speak and communicate the Orixás' words. This represents the last phase, in which the medium speaks directly to the clients or initiates to tell them the Orixás' messages and teachings. Their words are considered sacred and have the same value as a divine commandment, communicated to assist humans during their terrestrial lives. In some terreiros, these preachings occur through the words of the highest ranked figures in the Umbanda hierarchy rather than through the words of the mediums. Typically, these roles are taken by men in politics or those who rule the villages. These men often relay life teachings and norms, which will have the values of laws and regulations.

In this way, the terreiros are also utilized as places of political and social initiative. Through the presence and intervention of Orixás, these initiatives are turned into religious credos, which justifies their nature of absolutism. After such a detailed description of Umbanda's places of worship, some fundamental differences from the Christian tradition emerge, despite some apparent similarities (such as the meticulous use of water). The terreiros are not actual temples but rather open spaces: they are set up in the woods because such places are thought to be the most promising for communication between spirits and men. Inside the terreiros, there is no need for a real concrete structure, contrasting the Christian cult's large and magnificent churches. This is because Umbanda strongly believes in the direct contact of the body with the Earth and soil, which is the primary way of contacting the celestial world. This is evidently closer to the Yoruba tradition because the sky is directly connected to the Earth. Through their mutual union, man is connected to the entire cosmos.

CHAPTER SIX
Rituals and Ceremonies

Initiation Rituals

UMBANDA'S EVOCATIVE POWER IS ONLY POSSIBLE DUE TO THE expertise of mediums, priests, priestesses, and all the leading figures that practice this religion. This system is organized in a strict hierarchy, where members of one level can only reach the following one when they have achieved the intellectual development required. The passage from one level to the next is often marked by an initiation ritual, where the candidate is invested in the new responsibilities and provisions that the new role requires. Despite these rituals changing from terreiro to terreiro, there are five main important rites. This includes two initial ceremonies where the candidate is first introduced to the Umbanda doctrine. Two crosses are made on foot plants to promote a promising path towards wisdom and good for others. Baptism, analogous to the Christian tradition, is the ceremony that initiates the candidate to the practice of Umbanda. It is usually performed when the nominee is underage, and they are chosen based on the parents' affiliation to the religion.

During this ritual, the parents must be present only if the candidate is underage. During this procedure, the candidate is given all the energy emanating from the Orixás. The Cruzamiento is performed by the Babalao and consists of making a sign cross seven times in different places of the candidate's body. One cross is made on the forehead to promote knowledge and wisdom. Two crosses are made to chase away evil spirits on the heart and receive good spirits on the neck. After these two initial steps, the new Umbandista can start his formal training to become a medium. This, in some terreiros, occurs in specific rooms in which training the candidate is entrusted to a more experienced figure in the hierarchy who will teach him the laws and rules of his coveted position. When the initiated is prepared enough, he will undergo three more rituals that eventually turn him into a medium. The first of the two is the washing of the head. During this ritual, the candidate is poured water made of a mixture of herbs on his head to attract good spirits and withdraw evil ones. The second one is the coronation. Here, the Babalao puts a crown on the candidate's head and officially deems him a medium.

Invocation Rituals

All Umbanda rituals and ceremonies are held to create a connection between Umbandistas and the spirits. Like in many other traditions, Umbanda establishes such a connection through multiple offerings and prayers. Despite such ceremonies changing from terreiro to terreiro, the most widespread ritual is mediumship, where the spirits possess the medium's body to communicate with the clients. These rituals most often occur in terreiros (temples). However, it can also be practiced outdoors. This could include taking place in a forest or by the sea; however, it is contingent upon the most promising place for the Orixá to be summoned. Usually, the portion of terreiro reserved for the mediums is separated from the one reserved for the clients. In one area, the mediums make the consultations and assist a given client. At the same time, the rest of the terreiro is reserved for clients who watch the rituals and wait for their turns. The waiting clients are color-coded or name labeled, differentiating those who have already been initiated and the newcomers to whom a different procedure is reserved.

Mediums typically adorn white robes and protective ornaments, such as necklaces and chains. Mediums can have different levels of expertise and, based on that, will have other protective objects. Such objects are usually placed on a central table: disks and needles made of steel, rocks, caps made of glass, herbs, and seawater. The mediums hierarchy is established by Maes and Paes de Santos (priests and priestesses). Each medium must undergo complex and strenuous training to ascend the hierarchy. Despite such harsh apprenticeship, mediums are not regular people who choose this path. Instead, they are carefully selected before training, based on talent and proneness to mediumship detected by the priests. Mediums are fundamental for Umbanda, as communication between the two worlds would not be possible without them.

Before every ritual, there is a preliminary ceremony common to all Umbanda branches. They place flowers and seven candles on the central table and light it seven minutes before 12 o'clock on the chosen day of the ritual. At that specific time, the terreiro will be blessed with a prayer and the burning of incense. When the ceremony starts, mediums arrange in a circle and move in circles accompanied by the drums' sound and songs dedicated to specific Orixás. Here, a prayer entitled "Salve o Sahany" from Tupi tradition is recited. They continue to move like this, occasionally changing direction, until all of them have incorporated the spirit, typically marked by a loud yell from the priests. The second part of the ceremony is determined by the "Jogo de Búzios," which is a practice of divination through the placement of snail shells on the floor. Despite these rituals only being done to evoke the Good Spirits, the whole ritual process must be constantly protected and safeguarded so that external evil forces cannot penetrate.

For this reason, Umbanda magic is regarded as unique energy for protection. At times, they even hire special magicians, usually Tupi shamans, to keep evil forces away. In fact, the tradition of wearing protective objects and talismans likely comes from Tupi people, who were part of Indigenous tribes spread in different parts of Brazil. When the main ritual has finished, all the mediums gather in another circle, this time elliptic, keeping their arms crossed while waiting for the Babalao to bless them with incense. As a final thing, they all take the same position as a sign of supplication and devotion towards the Orixá. They will get down on their knees, look down, and spread their arms while singing a prayer three times to Oxalá.

CHAPTER SEVEN

Priests and Priestesses

Umbanda's Hierarchical Structure

UMBANDA AND CANDOMBLÉ, HAVING ESTABLISHED SPECIFIC religious systems, present well-defined hierarchical structures. These structures determine the relationships between control and obedience within societal and familial dimensions. A social scale isn't new: it has existed since ancient times, which was usually reflected in the specific structures in which families were organized.

Umbanda strictly differentiates between groups of followers and groups of leaders. It establishes rules for the management of relationships between these two ranks. On one side, the relationship between the followers and the leaders is based on family hierarchization. On the other side, we have the relationship between Umbanda and the exterior world, such as managing money and communicating with people who do not belong to the cult. Three principal figures make up Umbanda's hierarchical system. The three central figures are, figuratively speaking, of a familiar nature: father of saints, mother of saints, and son of saints.

It must first be noted that the hierarchical structure is based on a relationship of absolute intimacy, rooted in the terminological choice of Umbanda. A religious group is defined as a "holy family" or "consecrated customer," a detail that highlights Umbanda's tendency to consider its members in familial terms. From one point of view, the hierarchical relationships within Umbanda exemplify a family-oriented organization that one can find in every place and in any historical period. When speaking extensively about the children of saints, their primary role is to help the entire family. This is comparable to other family systems. Even those in which religion is not involved. An example of this phenomenon is how children were supposed to help their fathers work on the land. Umbanda's general idea of the family is that of a closed group dedicated to developing their own specific place free of monetary constraints, selfishness, and arrogance. This image dramatically reflects that of every family existing within a capitalist system.

Children of Saints and the Figure of the Client

When speaking about money within Umbanda's family system, it was not done to provide a random example but rather to mention a fundamental feature concerning hierarchy. The element of money, in fact, differentiates an Umbanda client from a son of a saint. This real difference allows us to insert the son of the saint inside the hierarchical structure with more clarity. The client is an individual who buys religious services of different nature by going to a terreiro to a specific religious family. This person is external to the family to which he asks for assistance and sometimes external to Umbanda itself. However, he secures a ritual by purchasing it with money. The service clients ask for are many; some include the distancing of evil spirits, search for luck and fortune, and blessing a son before birth. In Umbanda, it is very common to practice specific rituals upon request. Clients can have a ceremony advertised as "for sale" from a given Umbandist family.

On the other hand, the figure defined as saint-child or son of the saint is an individual who participates in the family nucleus as a financier or financial contributor for no personal turnover. This is a wealthy man who gives his money to a chosen holy family with the intent of seeing it grow and expand spiritually. For this reason, children of saints sometimes accuse the holy family they help to be exploiting them for their financial support. They would like to participate in religious ceremonies but are instead confined to the role of a "producer." Another fundamental difference between clients and children of saints is that the first is external to the Umbanda hierarchical structure. At the same time, the second has undergone the necessary initiation rituals to be inserted within the family. In this way, children of saints can be considered actual Umbanda members. Still, from a practical point of view, they mainly serve an economic function.

We can now highlight some important aspects. In Umbanda, a holy family identifies themselves with a given terreiro. Each holy family owns a terreiro with the money received by their children of saints. However, not all children of saints are considered equal. Despite the term "children" suggesting these figures are young, it is not a comparable indicator. There exists a hierarchy within children of saints based on their degree of spiritual expertise. The newly entered children are treated differently from the veterans. They receive more attention and teachings to better familiarize themselves with the social structure of their family and terreiro. There are also children of saints that provide financial services of a different nature. Some provide money, and some provide other services. Each member's hierarchical position within an Umbandist family is determined by their specific relationship with money.

At the lowest rank, we find the clients, then the children of saints, and then the father and mother of saints, who occupy the highest position.

Father and Mother of Saints

The father of saints is a fundamental figure in all African religions that dates back to before the slave trade. In fact, it existed before the African populations arrived in Brazil. It is not a strictly Umbandist feature, as it is also found in Candomblé and traditional animistic cults. Therefore, the "Pai de Santo" is considered the chief priest of African religions. He is a figure who, besides having the most direct and meaningful relationship with the spiritual entities, is also responsible for sacred ceremonies, purifications, and all that belongs to the rituality in both Umbanda and Candomblé. Clearly, the Pai de Santo is also in charge of a given house or terreiro. As such, it takes care of the finances, communications with clients and children of saints, and all figures orbiting around their terreiro.

The pai de Santo has a double role. On one side, he is a sacred place's financial administrator and organizer. On the other, he has the highest spiritual role among the incarnated. He is the most educated and cultivated. He is the closest of a given family to the moment of his new reincarnation. After all, given the centrality of his role, the Pai de Santo has several names. He can be called Pai de Santo, terreiro chief or Umbanda guardian. They are indeed guides: all people below them in rank must address their questions. Such questions can be of spiritual nature. However, they can also concern with other matters, such as what to eat to have a better diet or how to behave in certain family relationships. In Umbanda, many people want to become fathers of saints. This would allow them to start their own terreiro without being spiritually and economically subordinate to other fathers of saints. However, it is not always easy to begin ruling one's own terreiro, or "House of Saints." In fact, some priests can be judged for wanting to make a profit out of the religion when ruling a terreiro. AT times, individuals who are not priests will illegally self-proclaim themselves as the father of saints only to take ownership of the economic benefits.

On the contrary, the real father of saints has no personal relationship with money. He will only use it when necessary, such as in the growth of the terreiro. Moreover, he is a person who has no interest in everyday habits and society; instead, he is only interested in the good of the terreiro. This is where the principle of family community touches its apex. The Umbandista family is semi-communistic, where money is considered evil and is only used to provide benefits to be equally shared among the family members.

The position of the mother of saints can be considered equal to that of the father of saints; however, with one fundamental difference: she is a woman. Despite this, Umbanda has a different notion of gender roles than Western norms. In fact, both Umbanda and Candomblé treat the saint's father and mother of the saint as equal individuals. This differs not only from western societies but also from societies of Aramaic origins, such as Judaism, Christianity, and Islam. To reiterate, Umbanda members are considered more or less critical solely based on their spiritual advancement.

In speaking of Umbanda's relationship with money, it is worth noting that the importance and luster of a terreiro will depend on the resources it exposes during rituals. In this way, everything presented during a ritual, from the constructions to the quality of the offerings, will become the symbol of the ranking of a specific terreiro. Again, this demonstration of wealth is not about ostentation of richness but rather symbolizes spiritual power. It is thought that Orixás will be more likely to attend rituals in terreiros where many quality offerings are put forward. There has also been a comparison between the protestant conception of money and Candomblé's. The Protestant vision (Protestant ethic) has been analyzed extensively by Weber in his work The Protestant Ethic and the Spirit of Capitalism (Weber, 1905). There are communal aspects that allow an interesting comparison between Protestantism and Umbanda.

First, let us consider the similarities. In Umbanda, similarly to Protestantism, the individual is central and felt as a fundamental part of the universe. However, God has the ultimate power to decide which individuals will be lucky. By undergoing profound spiritual growth, one will be limited to their terrestrial sphere of sin, with no room for spiritual evolution. Protestantism follows the same school of thought: everything is attributable to the grace of God. In fact, Luther's thesis states that men's actions are unnecessary because God will choose who to save and who not to save. In both religions, the relationship with money comes from this same belief: having money and being lucky is a sign of having God's Grace and being chosen by him. According to Calvin, the possession of goods—such as having money and owning properties—represents being in God's grace and the salvation of one's soul.

There is a fundamental discrepancy in the differences between the two religions. Despite Protestantism equating the possession of goods with divine predestination, it emphasizes the importance for men to show off their wealth. Protestantism preaches asceticism, thus conducting a lifestyle deprived of any material richness. This is not the case for Umbanda, where the most important terreiros organize parties and parades to make offerings to spirits. To show Orixás their gratitude, Umbandistas show them material goods they have collected for them. This double relationship Umbanda has with money is intriguing. On the one hand, it is fundamental in promoting spiritual elevation; on the other, it is masked and rejected. In fact, terreiros that use the money to fulfill personal pleasures and desires are considered to be inhabited by evil spirits, where black magic is secretly practiced.

Conclusion

Because of Umbanda's popularity and the multiple facets that characterize it, it has often been classified as the official religion of Brazil because it places various credos and traditions into one unified doctrine. Umbanda syncretism, as discussed, appears to be a necessary but natural element, given that it arose from individuals of different backgrounds. In fact, it resulted from the blending of Catholicism (which plays a very significant role since it was introduced during the many years of the slave trade), the French spiritism of Allan Kardec, African traditional cults (such as Bantu and Yoruba), elements of Oriental occultism, and white magic rituals. According to the last official census of 2010, Umbanda was found to be practiced in Brazil by less than 1% of the population. This proved to be a significantly lower number of practitioners compared to the 1990s, in which more than 25% of the population was Umbandista. Given its multifaceted nature, this difference in adherence to the cult might result from Umbanda constantly changing, with many people worshiping their own versions of the religion. For instance, back in the 1970s, Umbanda eradicated the practice of animal sacrifice and everything that could jeopardize the establishment of

Conclusion

Umbanda as a legal cult. In this way, it distanced itself from Candomblé. If Candomblé and Umbanda initially only shared geographical differences, their belief systems gradually changed from one another. Candomblé is still very "African," in a way. At the same time, Umbanda has adopted different measures to standardize it in Brazil and make it accessible to anyone without fear of persecution.

Umbanda, in fact, gradually migrated towards the west, getting closer and closer to French spiritism and Catholicism and moving away from a strictly African tradition. Umbanda inherited the concepts of reincarnation and spiritual elevation from these doctrines through multiple incarnations. Especially in Brazil, this has evolved into the birth of help and support groups, whose primary goal is to help the poor. Another important difference between the two is the relationship with Orixás. On one side, Candomblé entertains a direct relationship with Orixás: the communication between humans and deities is natural, with no need for mediumship intervention.

On the other hand, we have Umbanda, which has created a complex ritual to establish a connection with Orixás. It is done through the assistance of mediums who, as we have seen, are highly skilled and spiritually elevated individuals. They have not yet reached the spiritual peak to enable them to be disincarnate. However, they are more advanced in their journey of spiritual elevation than normal humans. For this reason, they can communicate with Orixás through the momentary embodiment of the spirit inside their bodies and then distribute the spirit's teachings to the world. If Candomblé is mainly devoted to Orixás, Umbanda has a much more comprehensive range of spiritual entities it worships.

The lowest step in the hierarchy is occupied by the human figures of mediums. These talented individuals are inclined toward spiritual elevation. Individuals can only become

Conclusion

mediums when they have been elected by priests based on their spiritual talent and, most importantly, after undergoing whole initiation rituals. For instance, Baptism initiates the candidate to the practice of Umbanda, and Cruzamiento enables the candidate to start their apprenticeship as a medium. Mediums are fundamental figures in the cult of Umbanda because, without them, the practice of rituals and communication with spirits would not be possible. Next, in the hierarchy, we find the mother and father of saints. These figures are at the lowest ranks among all the disincarnated saints because they are still humans. However, humans are the highest ranked because they are the closest to reincarnation. They are in charge of the terreiro's management and handle the monetary supplies they receive from the children of saints. Moreover, we have learned Umbanda does not differentiate between the mother and father of saints because of gender, as the mother is invested in the same responsibilities and duties as the father.

Moving away from the human world, the hierarchy continues to grow with the figures of the Good Spirits. We have described the main categories of Good Spirits worshiped in Umbanda, such as the Baianos, Boiadeiros, Caboclos, Crianças, Exu (as a good spirit), Marujos, Preto Velhos, Zé Pilintras, and Pomba Giras. These entities are essential for their path towards disincarnation. They were once humans walking the terrestrial world and, because of their actions during life, achieved the level of spiritual elevation necessary to disincarnate and preach their teachings to the world. They are the ones who temporarily incarnate inside the mediums' bodies during rituals and communicate important messages to them from the higher ranks of the spiritual world.

Next, we find the realm of the Pure Spirits, which have strictly biblical origins. Among them are angels who directly accompany every human being throughout their life on earth. For

Conclusion

instance, they provide assistance by clearing the individual's mind when making important decisions. Lastly, the highest ranked are the Orixás, which reach their peak with Olorun, the God Creator. We have seen how the Orixás are fragmentations of Olorun, each of which represents a specific expression of God who would be otherwise unreachable. We have extensively discussed each Orixá and their particular contribution to the everyday world. On the other side of the spectrum, we have described the Evil Spirits, which Exu is part of in some versions of Umbanda. Overall, we have provided evidence of Umbanda's extensive versatility. Umbanda is a highly complex religion; however, it constantly evolves to be accessible to all, regardless of cultural background and race.

What's Next?

Discover the rituals, spells, and magic behind African Spirituality Beliefs and Practices.

African Spirituality Beliefs and Practices has long been the source of wonder. Movies and books and television programs purport to know everything about its beliefs and practices, but few seek facts, answers to their questions, or see it in practice.

The African Spirituality Beliefs and Practices Series aims to correct rumors, separate fact from fiction, and teach you everything you need to know about the many rituals, beliefs, and spells.

Learn more about African Spirituality with the other books in the series:

mojosiedlak.com/african-spirituality-and-tradition

Conclusion

References

Brown, D. De G., & Bick, M. (1987). Religion, class, and context: continuities and discontinuities in Brazilian Umbanda. American Ethnologist, 14(1), 73–93. https://doi.org/10.1525/ae.1987.14.1.02a00050

Carlill, A. J. (2013). Cherubim and Seraphim in the Old Testament (Doctoral dissertation, Oxford University, UK), 205.

Eliade, M. (1961). The Sacred And The Profane: The Nature of Religion. Harper & Row.

Engler, S. (2012). Umbanda and Africa. Nova Religio, 15(4), 13–35. https://doi.org/10.1525/nr.2012.15.4.13

Giumbelli, E. A., & Almeida, L. O. de. (2021). O enigma da quimbanda: formas de existência e de exposição de uma modalidade religiosa afro-brasileira no Rio Grande do Sul. Revista de Antropologia, 64(2), e186652. https://doi.org/10.11606/1678-9857.ra.2021.186652

Instituto Brasileiro de Geografia e Estatística. (2022). Ibge.gov.br. https://www.ibge.gov.br/en/home-eng.html

Kardec, A. (1862). Le Livre des Esprits: Contenant les Principes de la Doctrine Spirite. Didier et Cie.

Lanternari, V. (2006). Religione magia e droga : studi antropologici. Manni.

Lattuada, P. (1989). Sciamanesimo brasiliano : il simbolismo, l'iniziazione, le pratiche di guarigione dell'Umbanda. Xenia.

Oliveira, A., & Boin, F. (2018). New Age Umbanda: Axé and Energy in the Context of the Religious Transformations. Studia Religiologica, 51(4), 219–231. https://doi.org/10.4467/20844077sr.18.016.10100

Prandi, R. (2001). Exu, de mensageiro a diabo. Sincretismo católico e demonização do orixá Exu. Revista USP, 0(50), 46. https://doi.org/10.11606/issn.2316-9036.v0i50p46-63

Roldán, V. (2011). Valori, cultura e religioni : processi di globalizzazione e mutamento sociale. Francoangeli.

Weber, M. (1905). Protestant Ethic And The Spirit Of Capitalism. Wilder Publications. (Original work published 1905).

About the Author

Monique Joiner Siedlak is a writer, witch, and warrior on a mission to awaken people to their greatest potential through the power of storytelling infused with mysticism, modern paganism, and new age spirituality. At the young age of 12, she began rigorously studying the fascinating philosophy of Wicca. By the time she was 20, she was self-initiated into the craft, and hasn't looked back ever since. To this day, she has authored over 50 books pertaining to the magick and mysteries of life.

To find out more about Monique Joiner Siedlak artistically, spiritually, and personally, feel free to visit her **official website**.

www.mojosiedlak.com

- facebook.com/mojosiedlak
- twitter.com/mojosiedlak
- instagram.com/mojosiedlak
- pinterest.com/mojosiedlak
- youtube.com/@MoniqueJoinerSiedlak_Author
- bookbub.com/authors/monique-joiner-siedlak

More Books by Monique

Practical Magick

Wiccan Basics

Candle Magick

Wiccan Spells

Love Spells

Abundance Spells

Herb Magick

Moon Magick

Creating Your Own Spells

Gypsy Magic

Protection Magick

Celtic Magick

Shamanic Magick

Crystal Magic

More Books by Monique

Divination Magic for Beginners

Divination with Runes: A Beginner's Guide to Rune Casting

Divination with Diloggún: A Beginner's Guide to Diloggún and Obi

Divination with Osteomancy: A Beginner's Guide to Throwing the Bones

Divination with the Tarot: A Beginner's Guide to Tarot Reading

Spiritual Growth and Personal Development

Creative Visualization

Astral Projection for Beginners

Meditation for Beginners

Reiki for Beginners

Manifesting With the Law of Attraction

Being an Empath Today

Communicating with Your Spirit Guides

Life on Fire

Healing Your Inner Child: A Guide into Shadow Work

Change Your Life: How to Use the Universal Laws of Nature to Manifest Your Desires

Raising Your Vibe: The Guide for Becoming a Lightworker

Get a Handle on Life

Stress Management

Get a Handle on Anxiety

Get a Handle on Depression

Get a Handle on Procrastination

The Yoga Collective

Yoga for Beginners

Yoga for Stress

Yoga for Back Pain

Yoga for Weight Loss

Yoga for Flexibility

Yoga for Advanced Beginners

Yoga for Fitness

Yoga for Runners

Yoga for Energy

Yoga for Your Sex Life

Yoga to Beat Depression and Anxiety

Yoga for Menstruation

Yoga to Detox Your Body

Yoga to Tone Your Body

A Natural Beautiful You

Creating Your Own Body Butter

Creating Your Own Body Scrub

Creating Your Own Body Spray

THANK YOU FOR READING MY BOOK! I REALLY APPRECIATE ALL OF YOUR FEEDBACK AND I LOVE TO HEAR WHAT YOU HAVE TO SAY. PLEASE LEAVE YOUR REVIEW AT YOUR FAVORITE RETAILER!

www.ingramcontent.com/pod-product-compliance
Lightning Source LLC
Chambersburg PA
CBHW060819050426
42449CB00008B/1732